FORTRESS • 78

THE GERMAN FORTRESS OF METZ 1870–1944

CLAYTON DONNELL

ILLUSTRATED BY BRIAN DELF

Series editors Marcus Cowper and Nikolai Bogdanovic

First published in 2008 by Osprey Publishing
Midland House, West Way, Botley, Oxford, OX2 0PH, UK
443 Park Avenue South, New York, NY 10016, USA
E-mail: info@ospreypublishing.com

ISBN 978 184603 302 5

Editorial by Ilios Publishing, Oxford, UK (www.iliospublishing.com)
Cartography: Map Studio Ltd, Romsey, UK
Design: Ken Vail Graphic Design, Cambridge, UK (kvgd.com)
Typeset in Sabon and Myriad Pro
Index by Alan Rutter
Originated by PPS Grasmere Ltd, Leeds, UK
Printed and bound in China through Bookbuilders

08 09 10 11 12   10 9 8 7 6 5 4 3 2 1

A CIP catalogue record for this book is available from the British Library.

FOR A CATALOGUE OF ALL BOOKS PUBLISHED BY OSPREY MILITARY AND AVIATION PLEASE CONTACT:

Osprey Direct, c/o Random House Distribution Center, 400 Hahn Road, Westminster, MD 21157
Email: info@ospreydirect.com

Osprey Direct UK, PO Box 140, Wellingborough, Northants, NN8 2FA, UK
E-mail: info@ospreydirect.co.uk

www.ospreypublishing.com

ACKNOWLEDGEMENTS

I would like to gratefully thank the following people for their help in putting together this book. To my wife, Donna, for supporting and encouraging me with this project. To my brother Jim and Joe Kaufmann for their help and suggestions with the manuscript. To the Association pour la Découverte de la Fortification Messine (ADFM), the Amicale du Fort de Guentrange and Moselle River 1944 organizations for their time and assistance with my visits to Metz and Thionville. To Karl-Heinz Lambert for his valuable technical assistance. To the archives of the army at the Château de Vincennes in Paris, to Thierry Simon and to the Governor-General of the Army of Metz for helping me with access to the archives and to the forts of Metz. Once again, to my travelling companions Dan, Mark and Gavin for their company and their superb photographs. To François Hoff for his hospitality, for his excellent counsel, for his time at Metz and for the photographs he provided to me. To Marc Romanych, whom I can't thank enough, for his help with the manuscript and for the countless hours he spent helping me with photographs. To Raymond Decker of the ADFM, for taking an entire weekend to guide me through the forts of Metz, and for his passion for the fortifications. Finally to my good friend Jean Pascal Speck – without whom this project would not have been possible – for his help in setting up the logistics of the visits, for his hospitality that is second to none and for things I probably have no idea of that contributed to this book.

ARTIST'S NOTE

Readers may care to note that the original paintings from which the color plates in this book were prepared are available for private sale. All reproduction copyright whatsoever is retained by the Publishers. All enquiries should be addressed to:

Brian Delf, 7 Burcot Park, Burcot, Abingdon OX14 3DH, UK

The Publishers regret that they can enter into no correspondence upon this matter.

THE FORTRESS STUDY GROUP (FSG)

The object of the FSG is to advance the education of the public in the study of all aspects of fortifications and their armaments, especially works constructed to mount or resist artillery. The FSG holds an annual conference in September over a long weekend with visits and evening lectures, an annual tour abroad lasting about eight days, and an annual Members' Day.

The FSG journal, *FORT*, is published annually, and its newsletter, *Casemate*, is published three times a year. Membership is international. For further details, please contact:

The Secretary, c/o 6 Lanark Place, London W9 1BS, UK

Web site: www.fsgfort.com

THE WOODLAND TRUST

Osprey Publishing are supporting the Woodland Trust, the UK's leading woodland conservation charity, by funding the dedication of trees.

CONTENTS

THE GERMAN FORTRESS OF METZ 1870–1944

INTRODUCTION

After the Allied breakout from Normandy in July 1944, Lieutenant-General George Patton's Third Army advanced swiftly east across the French countryside. Its strategic objective was to advance through the West Wall, Hitler's answer to the Maginot Line, to the Rhine River.

In September, XX Corps approached the German fortress of Metz. American forces knew very little about the German position at Metz, in particular the forts that encircled the city or a smaller ring of forts that surrounded the city of Thionville, some 32km to the north. The American high command, including Patton, his staff and commanders, did not consider the fortress of Metz to be a serious obstacle to their drive into Germany.

On 8 September, the American 5th Infantry Division established a bridgehead on the east bank of the Moselle opposite the small village of Dornot to the south of Metz. On two small hills above the crossing point sat the Groupe Fortifié Verdun, composed of forts Sommy and St Blaise. The two forts were abandoned but companies F and G, 2nd Battalion, 11th Infantry Regiment, reached the barbed wire surrounding the fort, before pulling back when they received faulty intelligence the forts were occupied. On the opposite side of the hills on which the forts sat, the 2.Bataillon, 37.SS-Panzergrenadier

Caserne 7 of Feste Kaiserin in pristine condition in 1919. The structure in the foreground is the central caponier that defended the gorge ditch. (National Archives and Record Administration)

Regiment, began to move around the hills on the north and south to attack the flanks and surround the two companies. This serious threat, plus unrelenting German counterattacks and artillery bombardment, forced the Americans to fall back towards the Moselle River where they dug a quick defensive line in the horseshoe-shaped woods along the river.

In the meantime, the long-range guns of Feste Kronprinz (known to the Americans as Fort Driant), located about three kilometres to the north-west of Dornot, above Ars-sur-Moselle, began to fire on the 7th Armored Division units waiting to cross the river. Troops pinned down in the Dornot bridgehead were finally withdrawn to the west bank and a second crossing was forced a few kilometres farther south at Arnaville. The troops of the 5th Infantry Division managed to establish a bridgehead on the east bank, but fire from Fort Driant's heavy artillery continually harassed engineers attempting to build a bridge at Arnaville on which to bring across the armour. Major-General Walker, commander of XX Corps, ordered a general attack against the western and south-western defences of Metz, including an attempt to expand and break out of the Arnaville bridgehead. In the ensuing days, German defenders manning the fortress defences repulsed American attacks and the fort's guns kept up a steady fire.

On 23 September, the offensive at Metz ground to a halt, partly because of the stubborn German defence and also because the emphasis of the Allied strategy had shifted north to Belgium and Holland. Patton was permitted to continue 'local attacks', but not to make any move to encircle Metz. Major-General Walker decided to launch an assault to capture Fort Driant, which would help to open up the southern flank. An attack was launched in late September. After nearly two weeks of fighting, and with considerable casualties, the attack was called off and XX Corps paused to regroup. Fort Driant remained in German hands. The offensive resumed in early November and the city of Metz was finally encircled in late November, ending the battle, though some of the forts held out until mid-December. What was supposed to be a quick operation begun in September lasted more than two months.

Feste Kronprinz was built after the city of Metz became part of the German Empire. The provinces of Alsace and Lorraine were the spoils of the Franco-Prussian War, 1870–71. The Metz position, along with fortifications around

The barracks of Fort St Blaise of Feste Graf-Haeseler. The family crest of that family is above the entrance. The façade is of yellow stone, the original material used in construction. To the right is a chimney for the heating stoves. This was heavily damaged in 1944. (National Archives and Record Administration)

The elaborate portal entrance to Feste Kronprinz (Fort Driant). (Author's collection)

Thionville to the north, would form a 40km-long strongpoint, anchored by the Moselle River and known as the Moselstellung. It was planned as an integral part of Graf von Schlieffen's strategy to attack France through Belgium and encircle French forces from the west, using Metz as a pivot point for the armies.

The Moselstellung included 11 huge *Festen* or fortress groups, 16 smaller infantry strongpoints, detached gun batteries and hundreds of small bunkers built among the hills and ridges surrounding the cities of Metz and Thionville (known as Diedenhofen in German). The fortress was developed over a 45-year period from 1871 to 1916 and evolved from traditional 19th-century polygonal forts with open gun batteries to a series of fortified groups with separated combat elements dispersed among and blending into the surrounding terrain (a precursor to World War II era fortifications like the Maginot Line).

The *Festen* included infantry strongpoints to defend against an enemy assault as well as guns in steel turrets embedded in armoured batteries. The troops were defended from bombardment by concrete shelters. The whole position was surrounded by barbed-wire entanglements, ditches defended by machine guns and rapid-fire guns, all under the watch of sentries in armoured shelters. Underground tunnels connected each position. Electric lighting illuminated the interior and the troops had fresh water, ventilated air, heat, good food and clean sanitary facilities.

The concept was truly unique. When tested by the American forces in 1944, those defences that were attacked, from Fort Driant to the smallest bunker, held out against overwhelming force. And by that stage they were only a shadow of what they were intended to be.

An oval-shaped tunnel at Feste Guentrange. (Mark Bennett)

CHRONOLOGY

1864	In response to increasing tensions with belligerent and powerful Prussia, the French high command decides to modernize the fortress of Metz.
1870 – 4–6 August	After months of increasing tension, France launches an attack on German forces assembling near Saarbrucken. French forces are defeated at the battles of Spicheren Heights and Wörth and withdraw into France.
1870 – 16 August	German forces outflank Marshal Bazaine's troops west of Metz as they attempt to march towards Verdun to join up with other French forces. After the battle of Gravelotte (18 August) French forces withdraw into the fortress of Metz.
1870 – 27 October	The two-month German siege of Metz ends. Marshal Bazaine surrenders his 160,000 troops.
1871 – 10 May	The Treaty of Frankfurt formally ends the war with a German victory. A majority of the French province of Lorraine is annexed to the new German Empire under the former King of Prussia, now Kaiser Wilhelm I.
1871–96	Because of improvements in artillery technology the fortress of Metz is modernized and expanded by the Germans. The axis of defence shifts to face the new French border south and west of Metz.
1896–1916	To support a German offensive strategy, a massive fortress-building campaign is undertaken at Metz and Thionville to create the Moselstellung or 'Moselle Position'. A new system of fortifications known as *Befestigungsgruppe*, or *Festen*, are constructed and modified over a 20-year period.
1914–18	The Moselstellung is not attacked and the forts around Metz sit out World War I, encountering only sporadic fire from French and American artillery.
1918 – November	The end of World War I. In the ensuing Treaty of Versailles, Alsace and Lorraine return to French control.
1919–29	French engineers study the German fortification system and use many of its engineering design concepts in the Maginot Line. Several of the *Festen* are incorporated as secondary defences or command posts into the Maginot Line's main fortress line.
1940 – May–June	Germany attacks and conquers France in a lightning campaign.
1940–44	The forts of Metz serve as munitions depots and underground factories, barracks and training areas. Much of the equipment is removed and transferred to the Atlantic Wall and the Ruhr industrial region.
1944 – September	Patton's Third Army approaches Metz. German forces in the area occupy the forts and put up a stubborn defence.

1944 – 27 September –9 October	American forces are defeated in the battle of Fort Driant (Feste Kronprinz).
1944 – November– December	The Americans resume their offensive and encircle Metz. The forts surrender one by one. Fort Jeanne d'Arc, the last holdout, falls on 13 December.
1953–67	Canadian NATO forces operate out of the *groupes fortifiés* Marne and Jeanne d'Arc.

DESIGN AND DEVELOPMENT

Beginning in the 1850s, revolutionary changes took place in the science of artillery that resulted in an equivalent revolution in fortress engineering. In 1857, Prussia built the first artillery piece with a rifled barrel. Rifling, or the etching of spiral grooves on the inside of the barrel, caused the shell to spin as it left the tube, improving its aim, trajectory and range. Artillery fire could now reach the centre of a city from much greater distances than previously possible. Fortress rings built to defend cities from attack and to strike at enemy artillery batteries in the distance, had to be moved further and further out from the city, increasing the size of the perimeter and the number of forts. In 1870 the Prussians designed new types of fuses that could be adjusted to cause projectiles to explode at a calculated time, ideally over the heads of the defenders exposed on fort parapets. Without overhead protection men and artillery could be easily killed and destroyed by artillery fire. In a short period of time, existing permanent fortifications became obsolete and offered no protection for men or artillery.

The development that most radically changed fortress engineering was the 'torpedo shell crisis', or *crise de l'obus torpille*, of 1885, named for the torpedo or bullet shape of the new artillery shells. Not only was range and accuracy improved, but more explosive could be packed into the longer projectile, increasing penetrative and destructive power. Bronze shell casings were replaced with steel. Black powder was replaced with melinite, a new, highly explosive and volatile substance that caused significantly more damage to the structures of a fort. High-explosive projectiles were fitted with delay fuses that enabled them to penetrate up to three metres of earth and explode on the masonry vaulting underneath.

The barracks below the artillery ramparts of Fort Manstein – Feste Prinz Friedrich Karl – Mont St Quentin. The gun parapets are visible on the rampart. In between are munitions and infantry shelters. (National Archives and Record Administration)

Europe's military engineers undertook a number of studies and trials and concluded that concrete shelters and steel gun turrets afforded the best type of protection against high-explosive shells. In 1867 the French Army placed Général Raymond Adolphe Séré de Rivières in charge of the construction of eight modern, detached forts around Metz. Major elements of these forts included a bastioned trace with infantry parapets to defend approaches to the fort, a protective ditch and a central cavalier for long-range artillery. The fall of Metz to the Germans in 1870 and its later annexation provided the German military with an experimental ground for developing new fortress concepts.

At the outbreak of the Franco-Prussian War in August 1870, only four of the Metz forts were completed – forts St Julien, Queuleu, Diou and Plappeville. Two earlier forts that belonged to the original enceinte, Bellecroix and Moselle (renamed Steinmetz and Voigts-Rhetz), were upgraded with the addition of artillery cavaliers and casemated batteries. Construction had just begun on three other forts – des Bordes due east of Metz, St Privat to the south-west, and St Eloi to the north, which, after the outbreak of war served as intermediate gun batteries.

German fortress engineers built the Moselstellung in three major periods of construction:

The first period (1871–81) saw the improvement of the ex-French forts and the addition of new forts and intermediate batteries.

The second period (1885–99) saw the reinforcement of the existing forts with concrete, and construction of the first armoured batteries and interval shelters.

The third period (1899–1916) saw the development of the western and southern flanks with the addition of the new *Feste* design.

The left bank (see map of the Moselstellung on page 27 for location)				
Location on map	Original French name	German name after 1871	Dates of German construction	French name after 1918
1	St Eloi	Hindersin	1879–81	Gambetta
2	[German built]	Kameke	1876–79	Déroulede
3	[German built]	Zwischenwerk Tignomont/Schwerin	1878–80	Decaen
4	Plappeville	Alvensleben	1871–74	Plappeville
5	Diou	Prinz Friedrich Karl/Ostfort*	1873–80	Diou
6	[German built]	Manstein*	1872–75	Girardin
The right bank				
Not on map	[German built]	Batterie Kanal	1875–77	
7	St Privat	Prinz August von Wurtemberg	1872–75	St Privat
8	Queuleu	Von Goeben	1871–75	Queuleu
9	Des Bordes	Von Zastrow	1874–75	Des Bordes
10	St Julien	Manteuffel	1871–75	St Julien

*These two forts, technically a prototype of the first *Festen*, were joined to form the Feste Prinz Friedrich Karl (See glossary for terminology)

The 15cm howitzer battery of Feste Kaiserin. The façade is constructed in concrete and is most likely a reinforcement of the original stone. A caponier with rifle embrasures defends the gorge ditch. A spiked fence and wire entanglement surrounds the battery. (National Archives and Record Administration)

First period construction

Unfortunately, the construction records of the German forts at Metz are lost; however, by examining the forts themselves, along with detailed records of the construction of the other European systems, some conclusions can be drawn. The Metz forts were constructed similarly to the forts built by Général Henri Brialmont from 1889 to 1891 at Liège and Namur, Belgium. The earth was excavated, the combat elements were built and then covered over, and the terrain sculpted to military requirements. To build the concrete structures, wooden forms were used to build a shell for the footings, walls and ceilings, into which layers of concrete were poured. An examination of an unplastered wall in the sub-floor of the counterscarp coffer at Feste Luitpold shows how the concrete was poured in successive layers inside the wooden forms, a common technique used at the time. A wall in the flanking casemate of Feste Wagner that housed two 7.7cm guns, bombed by the US in 1944, is cracked at the joint where two layers of concrete were poured and where they perhaps did not join together properly. Once the concrete was poured and the walls finished with plaster and paint, the finishing pieces were added, such as windows, doors, embrasures, ventilation ducts, equipment, etc. Once the buildings were completed the landscape was smoothed over and banked for protective and masking purposes and the parapets and ditches formed. Finally, the palisades and wire entanglements were added. Photos of the construction at Feste Guentrange show a tramway system used to haul materials from the valley below. A similar system was used at Metz along with small railway lines for steam locomotives and wagons. There are some indications that labour was locally procured. Général Denis records in *La garnison de Metz 1870/1919*, that, on 12 April 1872, 1,300 workers were hired for construction at Feste Goeben. In 1889, 3,000 workers were hired from the mines of Saarbrucken to work at Metz. The budget for construction of the *Festen* was 50 million marks per year (400 million pounds sterling in today's currency), approximately 12 to 20 million per fort (100 million pounds sterling each in today's currency).

Second period construction

The forts the Germans inherited from the French were built of brick and stone, with minimal protection for personnel. The Germans spent the first few years improving the French forts and constructing new ones in the same style as other German systems throughout the empire – polygonal works with a bastioned trace, caponiers to defend the ditch plus open-air artillery and

infantry parapets on the ramparts. Brick and stone was also used to build these forts. The German improvements to the French forts included the addition of a wire entanglement around the works, a spiked palisade on top of the counterscarp wall and at the base of the escarp, infantry positions on the parapets, and interval batteries to augment long-range artillery capability.

The artillery crisis of 1885 forced the fortification engineers to modify the materials and organization of the defences to provide additional protection against heavy artillery. This marked the beginning of the second period of the development of the Moselstellung (1885–99). Concrete and metal replaced earth and stone. Concrete, a mix of Portland cement with stones, sand and water, was strong enough to resist the penetration of the high-explosive shells. In 1887, the Germans began to reinforce the masonry walls of the existing forts. Engineers experimented with a variety of combinations and thickness of regular concrete, sand and reinforced concrete. After 1914, reinforced concrete was used in all construction. It is possible to see the different stages of development in the various forts around Metz. Some of the buildings still have the original yellow stone façades. At others, the top half of the barracks is in yellow stone with window openings while the lower half is faced in about one metre of concrete.

A number of other improvements were made after the artillery crisis. Caponiers defending the ditch were replaced by counterscarp casemates and metal armoured observation cupolas were installed. Additional open-air artillery batteries were built in the intervals. A number of bombproof shelters were built around the interval batteries. There were two types: infantry shelters (*I-Raume*) and artillery shelters (*A-Raume*) for the men, and munitions shelters (*M-Raume*) grouped near permanent or field artillery batteries. There were 31 *A-Raume*, 32 *M-Raume* and 28 *I-Raume* in the first line of defence.

The most significant addition during the second period was armour plating. Major Schumann, one of Prussia's most prominent military engineers, who conducted numerous studies on fortress artillery, was the first to

The 21cm armoured battery between the Ostfort (Fort Diou) and Manstein, Feste Prinz Friedrich Karl. This is one of the first turreted interval batteries built at Metz in 1890. An observation cupola is visible in the background. (National Archives and Record Administration)

This photograph shows one of the first barracks designs built in the *Festen*. The façade was built of yellow stone common to the area. In some of the forts the stone was covered over by a layer of concrete. Final designs were built entirely of concrete. This is Barracks 3 of Feste Kaiserin. (Author's collection)

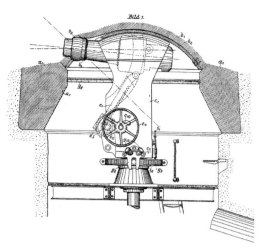

argue in favour of armour-plated gun carriages in revolving, steel-plated turrets to protect the gun and its crew. Schumann joined the Gruson Works in Magdeburg, Germany, in the development of revolving armoured turrets. In 1873, he invented a hydraulic gun carriage for a 15cm gun that reduced the gun's recoil, improved the function of aiming, and created a minimal embrasure. In 1879 two experimental cast-iron cupolas designed by Schumann, each with two guns, were installed at Fort Kameke, three kilometres north-east of Fort Alvensleben. Tests were performed in Romania on a variety of armoured turret models. Engineers concluded that a gun turret with two guns didn't work as well as a single gun, since the one gun firing threw the other gun off it's aim point. Schumann proposed large forts with dozens of turrets. Schuman's contemporary, Chief of Bavarian Artillery, General von Sauer, who also conducted many artillery studies, rejected the notion of a large fort, and proposed the organization of smaller, dispersed armoured works that would be less vulnerable to enemy artillery bombardment. Eventually, this concept of dispersal became a major feature of the third period of development (1899–1916).

Beginning in 1890, the first armoured batteries equipped with steel, revolving turrets were built throughout the Metz fortress line. From 1890 to 1893 two experimental batteries, each with two 21cm howitzer turrets, were constructed, one on the Mont St Quentin plateau, and one between forts Kameke and Alvensleben (Chêne West).

Afterwards, engineers came up with a standard battery that would later be incorporated into the *Festen* on a larger scale. From 1895 to 1897, the following 15cm armoured howitzer batteries were built (each battery with two single gun turrets):

Location on map (page 27)	Name	Location
S	Batterie Plappeville Norden and Battery Plappeville Süden	Adjacent to Fort Alvensleben
T	Batterie Chêne Ost	Between forts Kameke and Alvensleben
U	Batterie Queuleu	Between forts Zastrow and Goeben
V	Batterie Sablon	Between forts Von Goeben and Prinz August von Wurtemberg

These batteries were the final works of the second period.

Third period construction

By the end of the 19th century, significant work had been accomplished over the preceding years to improve the Metz forts. The perimeter of the forts surrounding Metz was 24km long and an average of four kilometres from the centre of the city, with 26 armoured turrets. However, the adequacy of the protection of the city provided by these forts was short lived. The increase in the range of artillery to ten kilometres made this line obsolete. An invading French force could place powerful long-range artillery on the undefended heights of the Moselle River nine kilometres to the west and range both the forts and the city without fear of counter-battery fire. In 1896, recognizing the potential threat, Wilhelm II proposed the installation of armoured batteries on these heights and in 1899 construction began on four new forts, to be called *Festen*, three on the left bank (Feste Lothringen, Feste Kaiserin and Feste Kronprinz), and one on the right bank on the heights of Sommy/ St Blaise, the Feste Graf Haeseler. In 1902, the Governor-General of Metz requested three new *Festen* be added to the southern flank – Feste Wagner, Feste Luitpold and Feste Von der Goltz – to augment the defensive strength of the position. Construction began on Feste Wagner in 1904. In 1907, an eighth, Feste Leipzig, was added between Lothringen and Kaiserin to bolster the western salient.

The *Festen – Befestigungsgruppe – Groupes fortifiés* (GF)			
Location on map (page 27)	**German name**	**French name**	**Year built**
D	Feste Lothringen	GF Lorraine	1899–1903
E	Feste Kaiserin	GF Jeanne d'Arc	1899–1905
F	Feste Kronprinz	GF Driant	1899–1905
G	Feste Graf Haeseler	GF Verdun	1899–1905
H	Feste Wagner	GF Aisne	1904–10
I	Feste Prinz Regent Luitpold	GF Yser	1907–14
J	Feste Von der Goltz	GF Marne	1907–16
K	Feste Leipzig	GF François de Guise	1907–11

Infantry works

In 1905, construction began on smaller infantry works in the intervals between the *Festen*. These included the St Anne Works to the right of Feste Lothringen; the Wolfsberg (Kellerman) Works; and the St Vincent, Leipzig and Moscou positions between Feste Lothringen and Feste Kaiserin. To further strengthen the western defences, several new infantry strongpoints were proposed in advance of Feste Lothringen – Fèves, Horimont I, II, III, the Amanvillers Quarry and the Vémont Position. All would include ditches, flanking casemates and personnel shelters, and be surrounded by wire. Portions of the Fèves and Horimont works were not finished. Finally, seven infantry works and strongpoints were built between Feste Kaiserin and Kronprinz – St Hubert, Jussy Norden and Süden, Bois La Dame, Vaux Norden and Süden, and Marival. Four infantry positions were added on the right bank in 1907 – Infanterie-Werk Chesny Norden and Süden to the north of Feste Wagner and

Feste Luitpold; Infanterie-Werk Belle-Croix due east of Metz; and Infanterie-Werk Mey to the north-east. In 1909 two infantry works were built in the interval of Lothringen and Kaiserin, the strongpoints of La Folie and Leipzig. These were connected together to form Feste Leipzig (more of an infantry work than a *Feste*, except for the inclusion of an armoured battery).

Infantry work – *Infanterie-Werk* (I-Werk) – *Principal Ouvrage d'Infanterie*			
Location on map (page 27)	German name	French name	Year built
L	I-Werk Chesny-Süden	Ouvrage Chesny Sud	1907–11
M	I-Werk Chesny-Norden	Ouvrage Chesny Nord	1907–11
N	I-Werk Belle-Croix	Ouvrage Lauvallieres	1908–14
O	I-Werk Mey	Ouvrage Champagne	1907–12
P	I-Werk Bois la Dame	Ouvrage Bois la Dame	1912–14
Q	I-Werk Marival	Ouvrage Marival	1912–14
R	Other minor works – St Hubert, Jussy Norden and Süden, Vaux Norden and Süden	Ouvrage St Hubert, Jussy Nord and Sud, Vaux Nord and Sud	1912–14

Interval batteries

In 1907 a series of interval batteries were built to the south and west to provide additional firepower and to command the lines of communications into the position. The guns were of 15cm calibre with a protected carriage *(Schirmlafette)* in the form of an armour plate placed along the front, top and sides of the gun carriage. They could be mounted on a railway car, moved where they were needed and installed in about two hours on permanent platforms. The batteries included munitions storage shelters plus a small command post and shelter for protection of the crew. On the west bank, from 1907 to 1908, four batteries were built; on the east bank an additional four were built from 1907 to 1913.

The positions during World War I

In 1914, Feste Luitpold and Feste Von der Goltz, and the infantry works of Horimont, Amanvillers, Bois la Dame and Marival were incomplete. Two additional *Festen* were planned to the north of Mey to close the ring, but they were not built as this was not a dangerous zone. Minor improvements to the *Festen* continued after the war broke out.

By 1916 the fortress consisted of eight *Festen* and 21 infantry works, and a total of 70 gun turrets (44 × 10cm and 26 × 15cm), and 131 observation cupolas. On the left bank, the distance of the forts from the city varied from 8.5 to 10.6km. On the right bank it was 7.5 to 12km. Three *Festen* and dozens of small shelters were built around Thionville to extend the Moselstellung to the north.

A 15cm Schirmlafette (protected gun carriage) cannon being moved by steam tractor. This type of gun was used in permanent batteries built along the east front of the Metz position. While the gun positions were permanent, the guns could be moved where needed by rail or along the roads on vehicles such as the one in the photo. (Association pour la Découverte de la Fortification Messine)

Festen at Thionville (all German built)

Location on map (page 27)	German name	French name	Year built
A	Feste Guentringen	GF Guentrange	1899–05
B	Feste Koenigsmaker	GF Koenigsmaker	1908–14
C	Feste Illangen	GF Illange	1905–11

Construction continued after the start of World War I. In 1916, after the failed offensive at Verdun, a vast effort was undertaken in the southern perimeter two kilometres south of the line Graf Von Haeseler–Wagner–Luitpold to build hundreds of shelters and combat positions in order to improve the continuity of the line and strengthen its defensive capabilities. These included concrete observation posts, machine-gun emplacements, flanking machine-gun casemates, blockhouses, bombproof personnel shelters, artillery batteries and special railway lines and military roads. Trenches and barbed wire further protected the main combat areas.

Principal features of the defence

The major elements of the *Festen* were the infantry works with large bombproof barracks, infantry strongpoints and armoured artillery batteries. In addition to the batteries and infantry works, there were small troop assembly shelters, blockhouses, casemates, observation cupolas and sentry posts. A field of barbed wire surrounded each *Feste*.

The infantry works and strongpoints were technically 'forts within a fort'. All of the *Festen* had one or more infantry works. For example, Feste Lothringen had one infantry work and one strongpoint, plus two detached infantry strongpoints. Feste Kaiserin had two infantry works and two infantry strongpoints. Some were stand-alone, isolated infantry works without artillery (Infanterie-Werk Bellecroix, Mey and Bois la Dame). There were different types of principal infantry works, from simple raised ramparts with parapets surrounded by wire and a fence to the large works with a ditch and counterscarp. The simplest works, infantry strongpoints, were installed in the less dangerous sectors and were cheaper to build than the infantry works.

The most important element of the *Festen* was the armoured battery. The design of the batteries was similar to the earlier, isolated batteries. The armoured batteries were equipped with 10cm guns or howitzers and 15cm howitzers. 10cm batteries were laid out in configurations of two, three or four guns per battery, 15cm guns in groups of three or four, spaced 20m apart (Feste Lothringen had the only six-gun battery).

A rare example of a forward infantry shelter near the Moselle River north of Thionville. Few shelters were as beautifully ornamented as this one. (Author's collection)

The batteries were built entirely of concrete three metres thick on the roof and walls, 70cm on the rear wall. The rooms inside the battery were on a single level and served by two corridors, one each in the front and rear. The combat corridor in the rear gave access to the turrets, workshops for munitions preparation, storage rooms, troop chambers, latrines and the command post. Munitions were stocked in the front corridor. The entries in the gorge were defended by a caponier at one end of the battery with embrasures for rifles and a searchlight. Wire and a spiked fence surrounded the entire complex.

Observation positions were scattered throughout the fort. Observers gave warning of approaching enemy troops or the location of incoming artillery and provided fire control for infantry and artillery commanders. There were several types of observation posts, from simple sentinel posts with a viewing slit, to more complex, rotating turrets with optical devices and flooring that adjusted to the height of the observer. In 1887 one of the first armoured observation posts was installed at Fort Manstein. Made of cast iron, several similar models were installed in the earlier forts. The Germans replaced these with a variety of fixed and rotating observation cupolas. These appeared in the armoured batteries in 1898 and later in the first *Festen*. They were typically placed on the high points of the batteries. The cupola was formed of a single piece of 20-ton steel, thicker on the side facing the enemy. The observation visors could be closed off with metal shutters. The observer sat on a rotating, height-adjustable seat and the upper compartment could be closed off with trapdoors to prevent explosives from getting inside of the position.

The Model 96 revolving observation turret was first placed in the twin 21cm battery on Mont St Quentin, then in the 15cm batteries of the first line and later in the *Festen*. The roof was made of steel, 15cm thick, weighing 4,000kg, and the interior had two levels. The observer manned the observation chamber on the top and a crewman in the lower level rotated the turret. The observer directed the rotation and the turret moved by slightly elevating it above the advanced armour to eliminate any friction. The floor could also be adjusted to match the height of the observer. The total ensemble weighed 70,000kg. In 1905, the Model 05 was installed in Feste Leipzig, the Kellerman Works, Feste Illange and Feste Koenigsmaker at Thionville. It was the same configuration as the Model 96 but the interior space was larger. It contained a telemetric device attached to a ring that could be rotated 360 degrees. The horizontal angles for fire control were determined by an index on a fixed, graduated rule; vertical angles were measured by the longitudinal axis of the scope. The observer sat on a rotating seat attached to the centre of the ring. There was a 60-degree angle between the embrasures and the observation field was 12 degrees.

Infantry exits, and picket shelter on the right, of the western infantry works, Feste Kaiserin. This magnificent photo shows the top of a principal infantry work in its pristine condition. The photo was taken around 1919 by American engineers studying the forts. This photo appeared in a *New York Times* pictorial series. (Association pour la Découverte de la Fortification Messine)

The observation cupolas also provided support for the infantry works. The first type was installed on the picket shelters in 1897. They were built in two pieces of steel and were laid out similarly to the models 96 and 05. Observation was by means of the naked eye or periscope.

Small sentry shelters were installed in large numbers to survey the wire belts and the infantry trenches. The most prominent version resembled a snail shell made of concrete or a double layer of zinc sheet metal with a bed of sand in between. The roof of the metal shelter was 5mm thick. It was surrounded by earth and offered sufficient protection against bullets, shrapnel and smaller-calibre shells.

Finally, to assure additional protection for the intervals, several of the forts were equipped with flanking casemates for two 7.7cm guns. These were placed on the extremity of the infantry works and consisted of a firing chamber, armoured observatory, command post at the foot of the observatory, electrical projector to illuminate the intervals, munitions storage and an assembly room for troops. Seven such casemates were constructed: two at Kaiserin, and one each at Marival, Wagner, Luitpold, Von der Goltz and Mey, plus four at the Horimont position. Five machine-gun casemates were built at Bois la Dame (2), Marival (2) and Von der Goltz.

TOUR OF THE SITES

When viewed from above, the *Festen* appeared as a series of rectangular concrete blocks scattered across a large piece of ground, tied together by roads and surrounded by a belt of wire entanglements. Each block represented a small, independent work, with its own access and defences. By size, the largest element was the infantry barracks, followed by the armoured battery, picket shelter, blockhouse, infantry exit and, finally, sentry post.

Infantry works

The infantry work (*Infanterie-Werk, Infanterie Stutzpunkt, ouvrage d'infanterie principal*) was an independent element of the *Feste*. It was preceded on the front (towards the enemy) and sides by a gentle glacis that sloped up from the surrounding countryside, obscuring the work from ground-level view. From the ground, the profile of the fort was minimal, except for armoured observation cupolas jutting up from the slope. The glacis was broken by a drop

The Seille Trench casemate, Feste Wagner

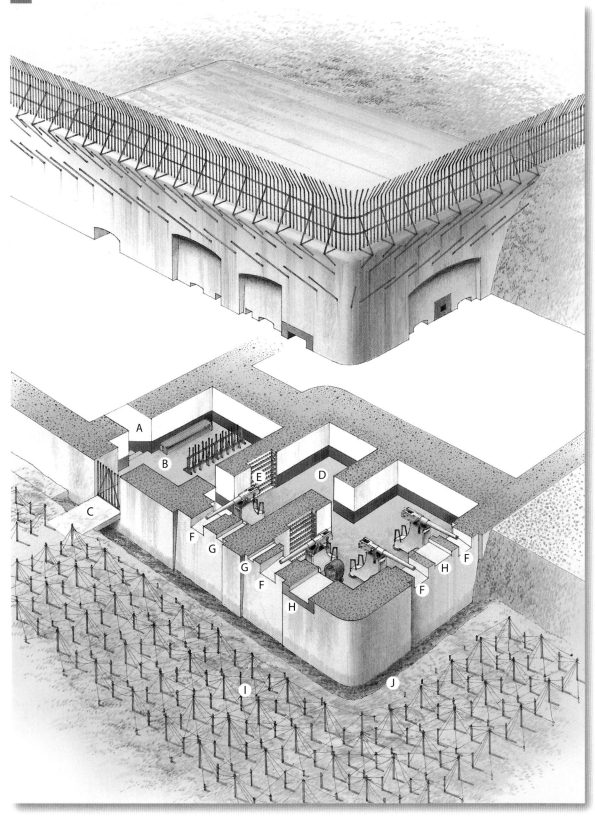

of approximately two metres into a 20–30m-wide belt of spikes interlaced with heavy wire that extended to the right and left (at mobilization, barbed wire would added to the top of the entanglement); this was studded with small metal or concrete sentry posts.

Across the wire the ground sloped steeply upward to an infantry parapet. The wire was under observation from the parapet that ran the length of what is known in ancient fortification terminology as the 'covered way', a pathway running along the perimeter of the position outside of the central redoubt. Along the covered way was a small blockhouse positioned on top of a larger casemate that defended the ditch (see below). The rear façade of the blockhouse was made of concrete and an iron door opened on to the covered way from the interior. From the top of the parapet of the covered way, the central part of the fort was visible. Behind the covered way was an imposing iron palisade, 2.5m high, topped by pinpoint iron spikes bent at the top in the direction of a potential enemy attack.

Beyond this palisade was a vertical drop of five to seven metres into a 10m-wide ditch that surrounded the front and sides of the work. A ditch always surrounded the infantry works; some of the smaller infantry strong-points had a ditch but most had only a belt of wire. The outer wall of the ditch, the counterscarp, was masked in concrete and the covered way and iron palisade ran along the top. Some *Festen* had galleries that ran along the interior

ABOVE
Concrete infantry parapets at Feste Obergentringen. A small bombproof personnel shelter lies behind the armoured door. This was the most intricate of the concrete parapets in the Moselstellung. (Gavin Saxby)

LEFT
The picket shelter of Infanterie-Werk Verny, Feste Wagner. From the underground bombproof shelter the infantry quickly moved to the parapets above. Note the concrete parapets and traverses to prevent enfilading fire. (Dan McKenzie)

A   THE SEILLE TRENCH CASEMATE, FESTE WAGNER

The casemate of the Seille Trench between Infanterie-Werk Avigy and the Seille infantry position, Feste Wagner. This casemate provided flanking fire with 5.3cm rapid-fire guns in two directions, down the hill to the Seille River, and along the access road. A – staircase from gallery to the casemate;

B – troop assembly room; C – exit door to ditch;
D – gun chamber for 5.3cm Krupp gun; E – munitions storage rack; F – gun embrasures; G – viewing embrasures; H – searchlight embrasures; I – wire entanglement; J – small ditch.

A ditch at Feste Kaiserin. The counterscarp wall is to the right, topped by a spiked iron fence. The escarp is to the left. The flanking casemate for guns and machine guns is in the back corner. The floor of the ditch is covered with wire entanglements mounted on spikes. (Association pour la Découverte de la Fortification Messine)

of the counterscarp, behind walls up to five metres thick. The counterscarp wall ran the length of the ditch. In the outer corners of the ditch were casemates with embrasures for rifles, machine guns, small guns and powerful electric lights. A belt of wire and spikes covered the floor of the ditch. Where the wire met the foot of the escarpment a second iron palisade, as imposing as the first, was positioned and it ran along the entire length of the escarpment. From its base the earthen escarp sloped upward at an angle of about 35 degrees. At the escarpment crest was a second infantry parapet more complex in design than that of the covered way that commanded the ditch and the glacis. This parapet ran along the perimeter of the central redoubt. The line of the parapet was broken by earthen or concrete traverses to prevent enfilading fire down its length. Small niches for ammunition were located below the crest of the parapet. Concrete platforms for machine guns were located along the parapet line. Built in the wall at the base of the parapet were small bombproof shelters to provide emergency protection from bombardment for the infantry. The shelters had metal doors to close off the entrance to the shelter.

Directly below the central part of the parapet was the picket shelter with exits to the outside ramparts. Staircases or ramps led up to the parapets. Typically, the rampart also had one or two small blockhouses with observation cupolas and infantry exits. Most of the above elements were connected to the main part of the fort by underground passages, though some of the smaller shelters were not connected to the tunnel network.

Armoured observation cupolas, either fixed or rotating or a combination of both, were located on top of the small blockhouses, the roof of the barracks or the picket shelter. These were placed on the highest points of the infantry works. Some observation posts with armoured cupolas were located in advance of the infantry works, wherever they could get the best views of the surroundings, and connected by underground tunnel (for example at Feste Wagner).

Barracks

To the rear of and below the central rampart was the barracks, the largest structure of the works. It varied in length and height. The front wall facing the enemy was built into the earth. The rear wall was open to the outside and faced away from the enemy. The gorge ditch ran parallel to the outside-facing wall of the barracks. The gorge ditch was a continuation of the ditch on the front and sides but had no wire entanglements. Across the gorge ditch from the barracks was an earthen embankment topped by a third palisade. In the centre of the embankment was a gap where an access road ran down towards the position. The roadway was defended either by a caponier in the centre of

The barracks of Infanterie-Werk Verny, Feste Wagner. The gorge ditch was defended by 5.3cm guns in the central caponier jutting out from the face of the building. (Author's collection)

the wall or at the end of the barracks, and/or by a detached blockhouse. The opening for the roadway was about five metres wide and steeply banked on either side. The roadway was blocked by another palisade with a gate for vehicles and a smaller gate for troops.

The barracks housed and supported a large portion of the garrison. It was a long building, typically with two floors and a basement. There were a number of entrances to the barracks located along the rear wall of the gorge ditch. During wartime all but two of these entries were closed off with metal bars. The wartime entry, located at either end of the barracks, was designed in the form of a 'chicane' in which the entryway turned to the right or left and the opening was guarded by a rifle embrasure and sealed off by a thick armoured door.

The layout of each of the barracks and armoured batteries was similar, yet each had its own peculiarities. Some of the barracks had two corridors, one each running along the front and rear; the earliest *Festen* had a front or rear corridor only. The hallway to the rear, which ran along the gorge ditch, was called the 'peacetime corridor' since it didn't afford as much protection during an attack as the hallway built against the earth, which also had a great thickness of concrete. There were a number of openings in the outer wall for ventilation and light that could also be used in wartime as rifle embrasures to defend against an attack on the barracks. The larger openings could be sealed off with metal bars dropped into grooves in the frame. In time of danger or alert the troops used the 'combat corridor' in the front part of the barracks. It was wider than the other corridor and there were no openings to the outside. The outer wall was built against the earth or the bedrock.

The floor plan of the upper and lower levels was nearly identical and consisted of a number of rooms that were used for different purposes. The floors, walls and ceiling were made of concrete and the ceiling was vaulted from side to side and sloped slightly downwards from front to back (reason unknown). The walls were painted white and some were decorated from 1914 to 1918 with stencils or murals. Most of the rooms were used as sleeping quarters for the garrison. At either end of the barracks, near the stairwells, were the latrines. The walls and ceilings of the corridors contained the ventilation conduits and channels for the electrical cables. Sinks for washing were located at intervals along the corridor.

Ventilation throughout the barracks was excellent. Small electric motors turned a turbine that drew air into the fort from armoured ventilation

The kitchen of Infanterie-Werk Avigy, Feste Wagner, with three steam pressure cookers and a hot water heater on the left for tea and coffee. (Dan McKenzie)

shafts located on the surface. The air was pumped throughout the barracks and the adjacent shelters. Each room had a valve that could be opened manually to regulate airflow. In the event of a shutoff of power, manually operated pumps were placed along the walls to keep the air flowing.

The kitchens were equipped with steam cookers, hot water heaters for tea and coffee, and ovens for baking bread. Many of the dining rooms, decorated by the garrison troops, had beautiful paintings on the walls that depicted idyllic scenes of the outside world, unit insignia or mottos, inspirational sayings like: 'Wir wollen sein, ein einig Volk von Brüdern' – We want to be a people, united as brothers – and other instructions and poems about beer drinking and eating. Water, fuel and coal were stored in tanks in rooms in the basement of the barracks.

Generators located in the power station provided electrical power. Most of these were located in the barrack structures, though Feste Von der Goltz had a separate building for the motors.

Deutz diesel motor that produced electricity for the Moselstellung forts (this one is at Feste Obergentringen). Note the beautiful marble control panel in the background. (Gavin Saxby)

B CUTAWAY OF A 15CM GUN BATTERY

A 15cm howitzer battery for three guns. The howitzer battery was situated on the back slope of the position so as to be masked from enemy fire. The direction of the enemy front was to the left, and this would be considered the front side of the battery, where the concrete was thicker. The battery was supplied with several peacetime entries along the rear wall to the right. These were blocked off in time of war and the angled entry shown at the bottom right was used instead. The door and grille at the bottom led down a gallery underground to an adjacent position. Each room served to support the fire mission of the battery. Munitions were stored in the hallway on the left, behind the thicker wall. Munitions were prepared in the rooms between the three gun turrets. The battery was provided with electric lighting, heat, hot water, latrines and ventilation. The ground to the rear was defended by a spiked iron palisade and a small caponier for rifles and machine guns.

15cm turret

Defensive caponier

Gorge

Peacetime entry

Projectile storage

Wartime entry

Barracks

| **The *Festen*** | | | | | | | | | |
Name	Guns	Observation cupolas	Sentry posts	Barracks	Men	Tunnels	Water capacity in cubic metres	Power of M – motor D – dynamo	Size (hectares)
Lothringen	6 × 10cm; 6 × 15cm	14	24	2	1,400	600m	2,036	M – 4 × 35hp D – 4 × 19kw	385
Leipzig	2 × 10cm	6	12	3	360	270m	324	M – 3 × 20hp D – 3 × 13kw	80
Kaiserin	6 × 10cm; 6 × 15cm 4 × 77cm	14	28	7	1,900	2,350m	4,570	M – 7 × 30hp D – 7 × 19kw	131
Kronprinz	8 × 10cm (with Moselle Battery); 6 × 15cm	16	29	6	1,810	1,500m	4,570	M – 5 × 35hp* D – 5 × 23kw	144
St Blaise Sommy**	4 × 10cm; 4 × 15cm 2 × 10cm	10 6	12 8	1 1	500 250		1,300 600	M – 4 × 25hp D – 4 × 15kw M – 3 × 20hp D – 3 × 13kw	45 30
Wagner	4 × 10cm; 4 × 15cm 2 × 77cm	15	51	4	1,250	1,950	2,200	M– 7 × 30hp D – 7 × 22kw	135
Prinz Regent Luitpold	6 × 10cm; 2 × 77cm	8	20	2	560	1,700	2,640	M – 7 × 27hp D – 7 × 18kw	83
Von der Goltz	6 × 10cm; 2 × 77cm	13	20	3	800	2,000	860	M – 4 × 22hp D – 4 × 14.5kw	205

*Additional 2 x 12hp motors in Batterie Moselle adjacent to Feste Kronprinz
**Feste Graf Haeseler consists of two forts – St Blaise and Sommy Works

Tunnels

Tunnels led from the barracks to the other positions within the infantry works and to the armoured batteries. Access to the tunnels was defended by a series of armoured doors and grilles. An armoured door was placed at the entrance to each tunnel. This normally opened outwards from the centre and had a small loophole at eye level through which a sentry could see down the tunnel. Several metres past the door was an iron grille. This provided additional protection and prevented any enemies reaching the door unobserved. Halfway down the tunnel was a second armoured door. At the opposite end was a grille and armoured door at the exit. The tunnels were about 2.5m high and averaged about one to 1.5m in width. These tunnels were rectangular, with a vaulted or corrugated ceiling, or ovoid in shape, depending on the thickness of the earth above. The ovoid shape absorbed shock better than the rectangular tunnels. They were lined with cables and pipes. Conduits underneath the floor carried additional pipes and cables. At either end of the tunnel was a small niche filled with explosives to block the tunnel exit if an enemy gained access. Smaller niches placed along the tunnels were used to hold petrol lamps if the electricity failed.

The tunnels also connected many, but not all, of the forts' smaller positions, such as shelters, flanking batteries and observation posts. Staircases or ladders led up from the tunnel floor to these positions. Each of these positions had an assembly shelter where troops waited for orders to man their combat positions. The shelters were provided with metal bunks or with hooks for hammocks for sleeping. They were provided with tables and benches for eating or for other activities to pass the time, and wooden platforms that hung from the ceiling to store personal belongings. The assembly shelters had latrines, ventilation and electric lighting.

Armoured batteries

The armoured battery was isolated from the infantry works as part of the dispersal concept. It was surrounded by a wire entanglement and spiked palisade. A roadway led down an incline to the rear of the battery to the building entrance with a gate blocking the end of it. Each battery had a defensive caponier at one end for machine guns and rifles, as well as a projector to illuminate the ground in the gorge. The battery was built on a single level. Like the barracks, two corridors traversed the length of the battery: the combat corridor to the rear (facing away from the enemy) and the corridor to the front (on the enemy side) where the concrete was thicker for added protection. Each battery had a command post for the officers, troop rest quarters, latrines, a telephone switchboard and workrooms to prepare and refurbish munitions.

The most important feature of the armoured battery was the gun turret. The cylindrical turret chamber was reached by a short staircase from the combat corridor. The turret had two levels, the lower level for raising the turret, quickly turning it, replacing damaged gun barrels and moving munitions to the gun located in the chamber on the upper level. The gun barrel rested in grooves on the inside of the steel carriage. The base of the gun carriage was mounted on a steel column that passed through the wooden floor of the top chamber and was anchored to a large screw in the floor of the lower chamber. The top of the gun carriage was bolted to a curved cap made of 15cm-thick steel that formed the ceiling of the turret. The cap and the gun carriage rested on an outer circle of steel wedges that were bolted together and embedded in the concrete surrounding the turret housing. (The French term for this steel collar is *avant cuirasse* or 'advanced armour'.)

The mechanisms for elevating the gun barrel to the correct firing angle, and for rotating the turret to the correct azimuth, were located on the outer partition of the gun carriage. The turret could be rotated quickly using wooden poles inserted into slots in the side of the gun carriage. A metal band marked with the degree coordinates was affixed at eye level to the inside of the gun chamber and was used to determine the azimuth direction. Once the gun reached the approximate direction, a wheel on the left side of the gun carriage was used for fine adjustments. The barrel was raised by a large wheel on the right side of the carriage and could also be adjusted to a precise angle

The lower chamber of the 10cm gun turret of Feste Wagner. The counterweight in the centre of the column eased the raising and lowering of the gun in the chamber above. The wheel at the bottom of the column raised the entire turret off its forward armour collar. (Dan McKenzie)

The gun chamber of the 10cm turret of Feste Wagner. The breech of the gun is visible in the centre. It rests in the gun carriage that is attached to the curved cap above. That rests on wedges of steel bolted together to form a protective 'collar' around the turret. (Dan McKenzie)

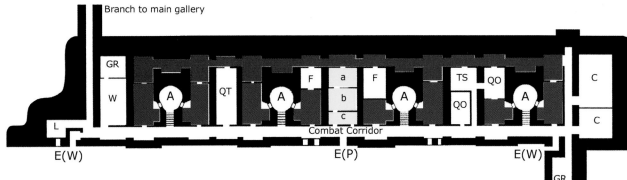

Branch to main gallery

GR						F	a	F		TS	QO		C
W		A	QT	A			b		A		QO	A	
L							c						C

Combat Corridor

E(W) E(P) E(W)

GR

Floor plan of a 10cm armoured gun battery.
A – gun turrets;
E(W) – wartime entry;
E(P) – peacetime entry;
GR – guardroom;
C – water cistern;
L – latrine;
W – workroom;
QT – troop quarters;
QO – officer's quarters;
TS – telephone switchboard;
F – fuse preparation;
a – spent shell refurbishment;
b – assembly room;
c – re-calibration room;
Red – projectile storage;
Blue – munitions preparation and assembly

by a smaller wheel on the left side of the carriage. The turret was raised by a wheel located at the base of the central column in the lower chamber. The wheel turned a screw that raised the turret several millimetres from where it rested on the advanced armour to reduce friction and enable it to rotate freely.

Munitions were assembled in workrooms next to each turret. Fuses were calibrated and screwed onto the projectile, silk bags containing powder were placed inside the shell casing, and the pieces were assembled together. Spent shell casings were cleaned and recalibrated so they could be reused. The assembled shells were delivered to the gun chamber using a manual hoist, where they were stacked in racks placed on the inside surface of the turret chamber.

If an electrical power outage occurred, the crews used petrol lamps for lighting. To reduce the possibility of fire in the munitions rooms caused by a flame from the lamps, they were placed behind glass plates in the wall, creating a barrier between the lamp and the powder.

The *Festen* had small sentry posts positioned in strategic locations on the fort's surface. The most unique design was a shelter built in a spiral shape that resembled a snail shell. The French called these *escargot*, or 'snails'. Some were made of concrete and some were made of zinc sheet metal in two layers, with a bed of sand in between. The small interior chamber had observation slits in the forward wall and sometimes in the roof.

A concrete 'snail' sentry post. Many of these were built of sheet metal and scattered throughout the perimeter defences of the *Festen*. The roof provided protection from small-arms fire. Note the visor in the right foreground. (Author's collection)

Map of the Moselstellung

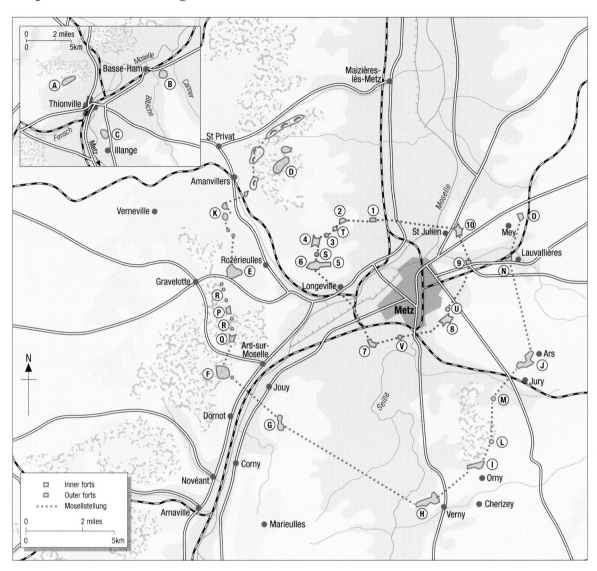

The entry to the *Festen* had no postern, drawbridge or outer wall, and simply consisted of a barricade guarded by sentries. The access road approached from the rear of the position.

PRINCIPLES OF DEFENCE

Colonel Pierre Rocolle, former French officer and historian, in his excellent treatise on fortifications, *2000 ans de fortification française*, describes the German *Feste* system as having a 'double originality' in the evolution of military engineering. First of all, the German forts were built to support an offensive strategy as a function of the future manoeuvre of the German Army in an attack on France. Secondly, unlike contemporary French forts that were singular, compact units inside a clearly identifiable perimeter, the German forts were spread out over the terrain to make them a more difficult target.

The Moselstellung at Metz as it appeared upon its completion in 1914. The city defended a vast network of roads, railway lines and river traffic. It was a key element of the Schlieffen Plan to attack France through Belgium in August 1914. The keys to the numbers and letters are in the tables on pages 9, 12, 13, 14 and 15.
Inset, the three *Festen* at Thionville, the northern flank of the Moselstellung. The city commanded the lines of communication passing through it into the heart of Germany.

In 1870, the German Army, still exuberant over the defeat of France, believed themselves too superior an offensive force to adopt a defensive strategy. The German high command planned to build two strong fortresses at Strasbourg and Metz for bases of operation during any future conflict with France. After their takeover of the fortress of Metz, the Germans built a new fort (Manstein) to the west of Fort Diou (Ostfort) on the Mont St Quentin plateau. A series of gun batteries, shelters and infantry emplacements were constructed on the plateau between the two forts, connecting them together to form an ensemble, or fortified zone. The result was very different from the French design, i.e. a polygonal fort surrounded by a ditch, and was given the name *Feste* in engineering nomenclature. According to Rocolle, the Mont St Quentin complex, named Feste Prinz Friedrich Karl, was nothing more than a 'rough draft' of what would come later at Metz.

From 1899, the new fortified works at Metz were a result of the adoption of the new offensive strategy of the German Army (the Schlieffen Plan) and became the strongpoint on which those armies would pivot on their march into Belgium and Luxembourg. Metz become the base of operations for the German Army's invasion of France through Belgium and Luxembourg, and the powerful line of forts was expected to deter the French from attacking along the traditional invasion routes into Lorraine while the German Army was mobilizing. The strong positions at Metz and the Breuchstellung (Strasbourg and Feste Kaiser Wilhelm II) in Alsace would force the French to attack a narrow gap in between. The secondary purpose of the fortifications of Metz was to defend the railway communication lines through which the bulk of German forces would pass on their way to the Western Front.

Metz

Metz is strategically located along the Moselle River, 56km south of Luxembourg City, and 48km from Nancy and Verdun to the south and west. The hills along the river are steeply sloped from Frouard above Nancy to Ars-sur-Moselle, ten kilometres south of Metz, where the riverbank opens out into flatter terrain. The hills south of Metz reach heights of 380m. On the left bank the escarpment follows the course of the river to Longeville-les-Metz. The plateau of Mont St Quentin above Longeville commands the river approaches, along which the major roads and railways run. At Longeville the Moselle straightens out and turns due north to Thionville, where it turns once again to the east into Germany.

On the right bank of the Moselle, south of Metz, the heights are lower than the left bank and flatten out north of the hill of St Blaise (360m). A series of crests run in an eastward direction from St Blaise south of the city then turn again to the north toward the Moselle. The city sits in a basin formed by these heights. Several small creeks and ravines cut through the heights on each bank and run down to the Moselle. On the left bank, the most significant creeks are the Mance Ravine from Gravelotte to Ars, Chatel-Moulins from Chatel St Germain to Moulins-les-Metz, and the Saulny-Woippy Ravine. On the right bank the main obstacle is the Seille River. Numerous roads and railways ran through the ravines and valleys and needed to be defended by the forts. The heights of the west and east bank formed the perfect location from which to command the entire valley.

From 1896 to 1899, discussions took place regarding the role of the German defences. There were two main schools of thought. General von der Goltz, Inspector General of Fortifications, proposed a continuous defensive line from Luxembourg to Strasbourg similar to the Séré de Rivières Line.

The opposing view came from Graf von Schlieffen, Chief of the General Staff. Looking to a future attack on France through Belgium, he viewed the defences as part of an offensive strategy, and proposed strengthening the fortified position at Metz (and Thionville) for use as a pivot between advancing forces in Belgium and a positional defence in Lorraine. The Kaiser chose Schlieffen's proposal, and the Moselstellung (Moselle Position) was developed.

Thionville

A key element of the Moselstellung was the city of Thionville, about 30km to the north along the Moselle River. Thionville is located along the Moselle where it meets the Fensch stream. The river is bordered on the left by gradual slopes up to 200m in height, leading west to the Lorraine Plateau. On the right bank the slopes are less considerable and rise to 60m. Ravines cut through the slopes on both banks of the river. The Fensch flows through a major industrial region that extends from the Moselle to the north-west. Thionville was a major industrial area at the end of the 19th century, with a population of about 14,000. It carried numerous important lines of communication, including major rail and road lines from Germany and Luxembourg towards Metz.

Thionville grew in importance along with the concept of the *Feste* system. Due to the distance between Metz and the French border, it was possible Metz could be outflanked to the north or south. The fortifications needed to be extended to prevent encirclement. The decision had to be made whether to place additional forts to the north or the south. Thionville was selected as being more advantageous. The Germans could take advantage of the natural obstacle of the Moselle to control the communication lines from the north. By building forts at Thionville, they could create a 40km front along the river. Beginning in 1899, three *Festen* were built around Thionville: Feste Guentringen, Feste Koenigsmaker and Feste Illangen. These were somewhat different from the forts of the Metz: the surface area was smaller, artillery power was weaker and the infantry positions were on a smaller scale as they did not have to defend against the flatter terrain found on the plateaux at Metz.

A Schumann turret at the Gruson Works at Magdeburg. (National Archives and Record Administration)

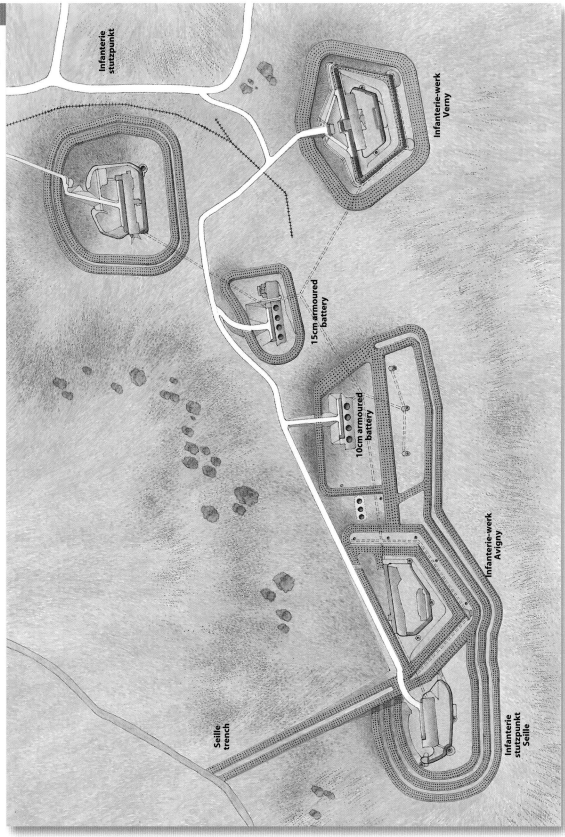

Infanterie
stutzpunkt

Infanterie-werk
Verny

15cm armoured
battery

10cm armoured
battery

Infanterie-werk
Avigny

Seille
trench

Infanterie
stutzpunkt
Seille

C OVERHEAD VIEW OF A FORTIFIED GROUP

Feste Wagner, between Feste Graf-Haeseler and Feste Prinz Regent Luitpold, south of Metz. This large *Feste* defended the beginning of a line of crests that ran from the Seille River in a north-easterly arc around the south side of Metz. It was the closest fort to the French border. The infantry strongpoint of the Seille, on the left flank, was built at a later time. It was discovered that that part of the crest blocked the view of the other works and also any enemy approach from that side. The Seille Trench casemate defended the rear of the fort and the narrow defile from the river below.

An AEG electric searchlight. The brightness could be controlled by adjusting the distance between two carbon rods through which an electric arc passed. A mirror in the back of the housing increased the brightness and the light could be focused with a powerful lens. (Author's collection)

Infantry exit of the Seille infantry position, Feste Wagner. The infantry parapets are above. (Author's collection)

Armoured batteries

In the 1880s, all the fortifications were in danger of becoming obsolete owing to the advances in artillery, and open batteries were extremely vulnerable to destruction. Existing fortifications could no longer give the batteries sufficient overhead protection to permit them to survive against artillery combat with mobile field artillery. Major Schumann, in his treatise *Die Bedeutung drehbarer Geschützpanzer "Panzerlaffeten"*, written at the Krupp proving grounds at Magdeburg in 1884, proposed the use of armoured batteries with steel turrets to protect the guns and crew.

A radical reform of permanent fortifications was needed. Schumann argued that the way to obtain the desired results was the employment of guns in rotating armoured turrets in place of fixed guns behind ramparts. Not only would the turreted guns be protected on all sides, but also directly overhead. A gun mounted inside a revolving turret has a 360-degree field of fire and is exposed only to direct hits on the gun's barrel. The field of fire of a turret-mounted gun is four times that of a conventional gun with a field of fire of only 90 degrees and no overhead protection.

The most significant and novel concept of the *Feste* was the separation of the elements of long-range artillery combat from the defence against infantry attack. This dispersion created multiple targets, each target with a smaller dimension, vastly more difficult to neutralize than the previous fixed fortress artillery designs. (For example, in the Brialmont forts of Liège and Namur, all of the guns were massed together in a central block, making them an easy target). This was a revolutionary concept and the Germans called it the *Panzergruppe*, later changed to *Festen*.

The *Festen*

The *Festen* were built on a large area of ground from 100 to 200 hectares in size. The various elements of the *Festen* were positioned to conform to the nature of the terrain and as a result were completely masked from enemy view. The defensive elements (infantry works and strongpoints) were placed in such a way as to be mutually supportable. For example, the distance between the artillery batteries and the infantry works did not exceed 700m and the distance between two *Festen* didn't exceed six kilometres.

The *Festen* were equipped with howitzers for angled and indirect fire (in other words, the projectiles were fired in an arced trajectory to reach targets that were hidden in ravines or behind an obstacle). Guns (not to be confused with howitzers) were used for direct fire. The main role of the gun would be to hit the enemy at the greatest distance from the fort. Howitzers had a more powerful charge and a longer range than mortars, were more precise and could fire shrapnel projectiles that rained down deadly fragments on the exposed enemy troops.

A 15cm howitzer turret. Note how it is raised several centimetres above the surrounding armour (embedded below the concrete). This reduced friction so the turret could revolve more freely. (Author's collection)

The *Festen* also needed to be defended against an infantry attack to capture the fort. This defence of the approaches to the fort included the principal infantry work (*Hauptinfanteriewerk*), infantry strongpoints and firing trenches. These types of defensive positions were placed on the perimeter of the *Feste*. The infantry garrison was housed in bombproof barracks with a central redoubt. The combat elements were linked together by an underground passage, flanked and protected by a deep ditch, an imposing, spiked palisade and, finally, by a thick belt of wire around the perimeter. Ditches with a counterscarp wall were defended by concrete casemates equipped with rapid-fire guns, machine guns and rifles, and illuminated by powerful electric lights. Camouflage was provided by false batteries, cover of the observatories with vegetation, and use of the natural terrain. The passive shelters – barracks, observation posts and combat shelters – were also dispersed to make them more difficult to strike, and to fulfil their functions as troop shelters and combat support for the armoured batteries and infantry works.

Command and control was assured by a system of observation and redundant communications. Observatories were placed on the high points of the fort in armoured cupolas equipped with the latest optical equipment – binoculars, periscopes and telemetry scopes. From these locations, observers could provide information to infantry or artillery commanders. If the observer spotted a target, he communicated via acoustic tube to telephone operators who relayed messages and alerts to the commander. Infantry observers also relayed target coordinates directly to the gunners defending the flanking casemates of the infantry works, or to the operators of the projectors used to illuminate the ground surrounding the work. A series of alarms signalled an attack to the infantry troops waiting in shelters.

In the event of an alarm, the infantrymen picked up rifles and ammunition, moved quickly out of the assembly shelter, opened the armoured doors to the outside and proceeded up a staircase or ramp to the infantry parapets on the top of the fort. Machine-gun teams set up their Maxim machine guns on special platforms along the parapet. In case of bombardment the troops manning the parapets ran for cover in the shelter. If they were unable to reach the main shelter, there were smaller shelters built along the base of the parapet.

After studying the effects of countermining during the siege of Port Arthur in the Russo-Japanese War of 1904–05, countermine galleries were added for additional protection against enemy infiltration into the tunnels. Rooms adjacent to the countermine tunnels had false floors that could be removed to reveal a deep pit below the floor that could be filled with the excavated dirt. The tunnels were started to a length of about four metres and capped with concrete. If needed, the concrete would be broken and the earth excavated and dumped into the space below the false floor. Based on the volume of empty space below the floor, tunnels could be dug to a total length of 35–50m.

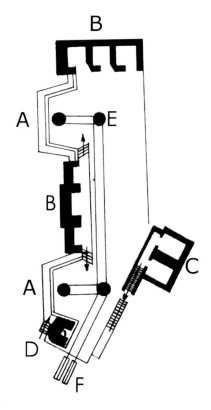

The Batterie Chatel St Germain.
A – gun battery for 15cm gun;
B – munitions storage;
C – command post and shelter;
D – defensive casemate;
E – turntable for guns;
F – railway terminus.

D NEXT PAGE: INFANTERIE-WERK VERNY, FESTE WAGNER

This was the 'fort within a fort' that guarded the approaches to the *Feste*. A – perimeter wire entanglement; B – entry gate and access road; C – blockhouse; D – gorge ditch; E – central caponiers; F – barracks; G – ditch; H – counterscarp wall; I – flanking ditch casemates; J – covered way; K – infantry parapets; L – picket shelter; M – infantry exit with observation cupola; N – glacis

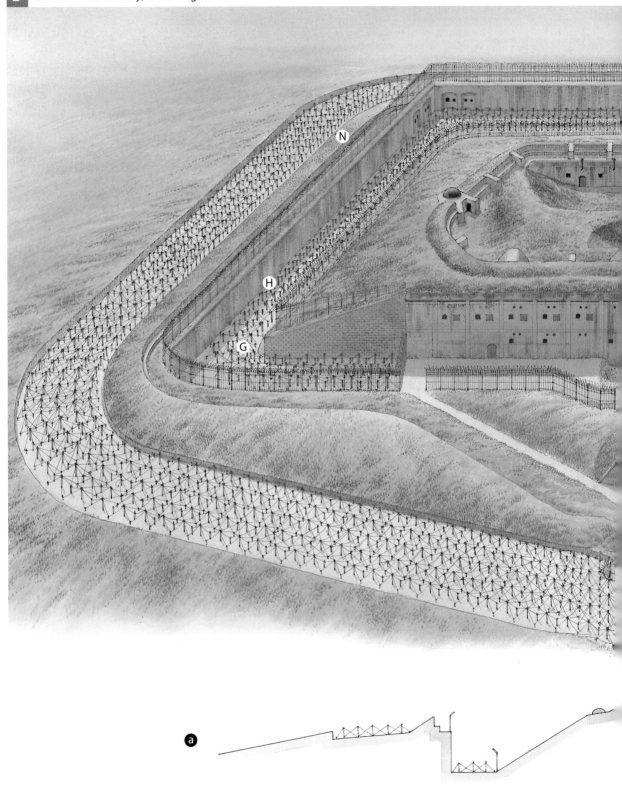

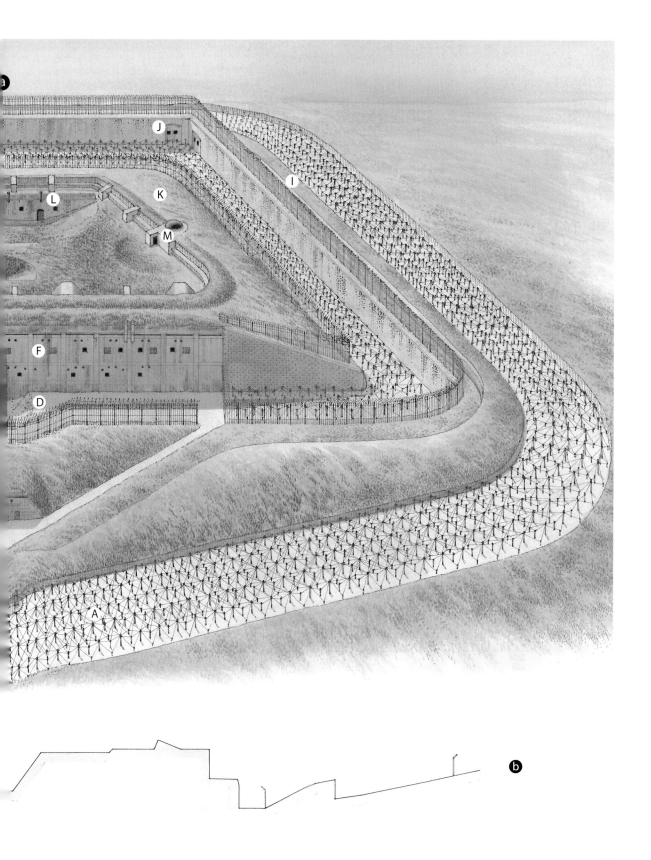

The defence of the entire fortress line was complemented by interval artillery batteries with mobile 15cm guns mounted on armoured carriages (*Schirmlaffettenbatterien* – SLB). The maximum range of the Model 1903 gun was 15.5km. The range of the Model 1916 was 19.6km. The role of the interval artillery was to assist in the interdiction of the railways and principal roads into Metz. Each battery was a permanent work built in concrete with two gun positions, munitions storage and a command post shelter. The guns were mobile and could be moved forwards where they were needed the most. Eight guns of this type were stored in a military depot for rapid deployment. The guns could be placed on railway cars and moved to their new location, dismounted and set up on the concrete emplacement. It took a small crew about two hours to set up the guns.

Hundreds of small works – infantry shelters, command posts, munitions shelters and observation posts – were built to the south of Metz between Marieulles and Cherizey. The terrain in this region is a series of successive crests preceding the heights occupied by Feste Wagner and Feste Luitpold. The purpose of the works was to create an advanced position of defence in one of the more vulnerable sectors and to provide a point for forces to fall back on in case of a collapse of the front. This forward line was a mix of different works of differing design and strength. The line was first designed to have small rest and combat shelters to defend against small-calibre fire. Carefully sited trenches and machine-gun positions were placed throughout. Later on, a successive line was developed to include a first, second and third line of trenches. Their numbers appeared out of proportion with the number of troops available to occupy them. The purpose of this was to mask the most strongly occupied sectors of the terrain from the enemy. The shelters presented a linked network, with no discernable break, located along the most important points of the terrain, giving the defender several advantages. Aerial observation was not able to separate the heavily occupied zones from those partially occupied as the density of the shelters was consistent throughout the zone. Also, spies could not distinguish the more heavily from the less heavily defended zones and if a shelter was destroyed in a radius of 30m there was another for the soldiers to use.

THE LIVING SITES

The forts of Metz and Thionville were noteworthy in that they experienced only a short period of intense combat, from September to November 1944. They were placed on a war footing in anticipation of a possible French offensive in the direction of Metz in August 1914, and were lightly garrisoned throughout the war as manpower was needed elsewhere along the front. They were used sparingly by the French in 1939–40 and abandoned after the German conquest of France, being used mostly for storage and spare parts. After World War II some of the forts were used until 1967 by NATO forces, after which time they were mostly abandoned.

During the Franco-Prussian War, from November 1870 after the surrender of Marshal Bazaine's forces to the Germans, Metz became a transit point for German troops on their way to battle. Convoy after convoy passed through Metz. The first large unit to call Metz home was the 3rd Reserve Division. By May 1871, approximately 10,000 troops garrisoned the fortress, and in June, a permanent garrison had established itself at Fort Moselle.

Many German recruits, including the fortress troops, received their training at the Metz encampments. Recruitment and training were tough, strict and very regimented. The troops' hours were occupied with drill, manoeuvres, exercises, parades, medal ceremonies and inspections. Kaiser Wilhelm II passed through the city on numerous occasions, as did many other German dignitaries. A typical duty day for an artillery regiment was as follows:

0545hrs – instruction for gunners
0700–1200hrs – instruction for the battery
1300–1500hrs – grooming horses and cleaning of the guns
1600hrs – inspection of material
1700–1800hrs – instruction in quarters
2200hrs – retreat

Artillery and shooting practice with live rounds took place at Hagenau in Alsace and Elsenborn near Belgium.

The soldiers enjoyed a great deal of camaraderie off duty, and the different units mixed freely. Officers joined together in pubs, cafés and garden parties. They attended the theatre and concerts on the esplanade by the Moselle. A favourite practice of General Haeseler was to call for alert drills very early in the morning after a festive night.

In July 1914 a 'state of danger of war' (*Kriegsgefahr*) was declared and mobilization of the Germany Army began. The forts received their wartime contingents in late July. The older classes formed the reserve contingents and the 33rd Reserve Division was assigned to guard Metz. As war approached the town began to swell with soldiers, many destined for the front lines. Units left the casernes in the city for their places of duty in the *Festen*, smaller works and interval positions. Along the way, women served chocolate, coffee, lemonade, sausage, ham and bread. For the first time the forts were manned by their full garrisons.

A French soldier monitors the electrical control panel in a *Feste* power station. The location is unknown; however, based on the complexity of the board it is one of the largest *Festen*. (Marc Romanych)

The entrance road leading to the western infantry works of Feste Kaiserin. The central caponier of Caserne 7 is visible beyond the gate. The infantry parapets can be seen on top of the caserne. (National Archives and Record Administration)

German soldiers in a fort at Metz, possibly Fort Manstein. They are standing in a parade ground in front of the main barracks building. This photo would have been taken after August 1914 since before that time, German troops would have been garrisoned within the city. (Association pour la Découverte de la Fortification Messine)

The forts were occupied by the garrison of Metz under General von Oven. Generalleutnant von Lochow was in charge of forces at Thionville. His command post was at Feste Illangen.

The infantry troops were housed in the large barracks buildings of the principal infantry works or in the smaller interval positions. A soldier was assigned to a sleeping location in one of the many rooms inside the barracks. He was issued a hammock which, when it was time to sleep, was hung between hooks attached to the ceiling and walls of the room. In some of the forts the men slept on metal bunks. Officers slept on bunks in smaller quarters with fewer men per room. Because they were made of concrete and below ground, the rooms were cool in the summer. On cold days a soldier was assigned the task of keeping the coal fire going in a small stove that heated the room. The coal was stored in the lower floor of the barracks. Smoke from the fire went out through vents in the ceiling. Most of the forts had coal stoves; however, some of the later forts had central heating and required a round-the-clock crew to keep the boilers operating. The boilers heated water that was pumped by electric motor throughout the fort.

The sanitary facilities were good, with hot and cold running water, and sewers under the latrines. The men washed in basins located in the corridors throughout the barracks. Feste Guentringen has a unique example of a shower room with brass showerheads and fixtures to control the temperature of the water. Water came from wells beneath the fort or piped in from the nearest civilian source.

Each fort had chefs and bakers. Each day the bakers fired up the baking ovens and used mixers to knead the dough

Hammocks used in the sleeping quarters of the troops. The ropes were strung across the room and attached to hooks in the wall and ceiling. (Author's collection)

A forward troop assembly shelter near one of the exits to the infantry parapets. The undulating sheet metal ceiling prevented concrete dust from falling on the troops and equipment. (Dan McKenzie)

necessary to make the dozens of loaves of bread required each day. In the kitchens, chefs mixed all sorts of meats and vegetables in large pressure cookers. The regular troops entered a queue to get their food and ate in the troop chambers. The officers were served by stewards and ate in a dining room, often decorated with murals. For those men serving in the more remote locations of the forts, their assembly shelters were supplied with coal stoves that provided heat and included a small reservoir on top that could be filled with water to keep their food containers warm. Either the food would be delivered or someone would be given the duty of picking it up from the kitchen.

The electricians were responsible for maintaining the electrical systems. Generators powered the forts if electricity from the outside was cut. A full crew worked in the power station to maintain and operate the diesel motors and dynamos. Continued maintenance was necessary to keep the machinery working in top condition. The machines were frequently lubricated, adjusted and repaired, and parts were replaced. Depending on the needs of the garrison, one or more of the motors was generating electricity at all times. An engineer controlled the distribution of the current on a large marble panel, adjusting switches and maintaining a written daily historical log of events. Other members of the crew inspected and repaired electrical and communications wire that ran in conduits throughout the buildings and tunnels. Each building had a workshop for equipment repair.

When not on duty, the men and officers would write letters, read books, share stories and jokes, and play games or cards. The officers might retire to the canteen to drink beer or wine. It was inevitable that a soldier would get sick or injured and spend time in the infirmary. On occasion soldiers

An example of one of the many murals painted on the walls inside Feste Luitpold, in itself a veritable art gallery of military murals. There are some quite fascinating pieces of art, still in excellent condition yet under no protection from vandalism. (Author's collection)

were granted leave to go home and visit their families. Fortress duty was specialized and it was important to keep the garrison healthy and highly trained.

The garrison was given duties patrolling the outlying areas of the works. A duty roster was kept at all times indicating a soldier's assigned position. Troops manned the picket shelters, blockhouses and counterscarp casemates at all times. While they didn't stand all day in front of an embrasure with rifle at the ready, since there would be ample time to move to that position in case of alarm, they stayed in the vicinity of their post, ready to respond to any warning. The daily routine was tedious, mostly consisting of sitting and waiting. If the troops were lucky, the commander would give them practice drills and alerts, and based on the written record, this was done quite often in the Imperial Army. Sentry duty was assigned on a rotating basis. Sentries were positioned in posts along the perimeter wire and in foot patrols around the fort. The duty must have been a lonely one, especially on a dark and cold night.

The heart of the fort was the armoured gun battery. Men from the artillery regiments were assigned to operate the turret guns. Crews of eight men worked the 10cm gun turrets; 15cm turrets had a crew of five. These included the gun officer or corporal, canoniers in the gun chamber to manoeuvre, load and fire the guns, and munitions servicemen in the lower chamber to maintain the stock of munitions and raise the gun for firing. Men also prepared and refurbished the shells in the munitions workrooms adjacent to the turrets. The battery commander and his staff were assigned a room in the block in which they worked, slept and ate.

Over time, the lack of action led to a relaxation of the atmosphere in the forts. As the threat of battle lessened, soldiers were pulled out of duty to build the advanced positions, and some units were rotated to the front lines. Skeleton or maintenance crews may have manned certain forts. The reality of a large *Feste* with its complete contingent of 1,200 men manning every duty position and gun at all times did not happen. In early November 1918 the forts were completely abandoned and served as storage depots in the 1920s and 1930s.

As war with Hitler drew near, some of the forts of the Moselstellung were assigned as a backup position to the Maginot Line. The former Feste Kaiserin, renamed Groupe Fortifié Jeanne d'Arc by the French, served as headquarters for the French Third Army. From there, in early June 1940, as the Germans closed in from the west, the orders were given to abandon and sabotage the forts of the Maginot Line. During World War II the German Army used the Metz forts for storage.

If the crews in the forts in 1916 were skeletal, it was nothing compared to what

French troops belonging to the 165e Régiment d'Artillerie de Position man the 'Maginot Line', as indicated on the caption to this photo. It is actually the Ouvrage d'Ars-Laquenexy, Groupe Fortifié Marne. (Association pour la Découverte de la Fortification Messine)

LA LIGNE MAGINOT
3. Soldats arrivant aux casemates. Soldiers reaching a fortress

faced General Patton's Third Army as he approached Metz in September 1944. It must have been an odd situation indeed for the German defenders of Metz to be thrown inside a concrete fort and find their way around the dark tunnels and overgrown surface covered with hidden, dangerous spikes and obstacles. Yet, the defenders managed quite well to set up a solid defence, put parts of the forts in working order, and harass and delay the overwhelmingly superior US force.

Engineers were sent to Metz to put the guns in working order. The *Volksgrenadieren* were thrown quickly into the sentry positions and shelters. Some were chosen, perhaps with artillery experience, to man the turrets. Doubtless, the command and fire control was nothing approaching the precision intended, yet it was effective. The troops sent to Metz had little time to think, and in the days before the battle began, they thought only of their main purpose, to make a stand and defend every inch of ground as long as possible.

In the 1950s the forts took on a different, more modern role. The Groupes Fortifiés Marne and Jeanne d'Arc were occupied by Canadian, US and French Air Force communications troops assigned to NATO. They lived in barracks in the city or at the Château de Mercy and drove back and forth to work each day. The façade of the barracks of the infantry works of the Gruppe Ars-Laquenexy (Ouvrage d'Ars-Laquenexy of Groupe Fortifié Marne) still carries vestiges of white signs with black lettering used to identify parking spaces in front of the building. Communications and signals specialists, both military and civilian, manned the command centre inside. While not providing the comforts of home, the barracks were modified and updated for their new, if temporary occupants.

A German officer arrives at Fort St Blaise. The forts of Metz were very sparsely inhabited up until Patton's approach to Metz in late August 1944. Hitler ordered the forts to be garrisoned and made operational and be held till the last man. (Association pour la Découverte de la Fortification Messine)

THE SITES AT WAR

The history of the Moselstellung is unusual in that it was built in the late 1800s by Germans to defend against a French attack from the west; later, after World War I, it was incorporated by the French into the Maginot Line to defend against a German attack from the east, and it was finally employed in 1944 by a retreating German army to defend against an American attack from the west.

During World War I the Moselstellung was a powerful deterrent to a French attack. It was what the French later hoped the Maginot Line would be. It was not attacked or even threatened by the French. In 1940 a German attack on the Maginot defences of the Région Fortifié de Metz was not contemplated. It was not until 1944, some 30 years after they were completed, that the forts, which at the time were a shell of their former state, would be put to the test of combat. They performed well during the battle for Metz in 1944 and

Map of the American attack on Metz

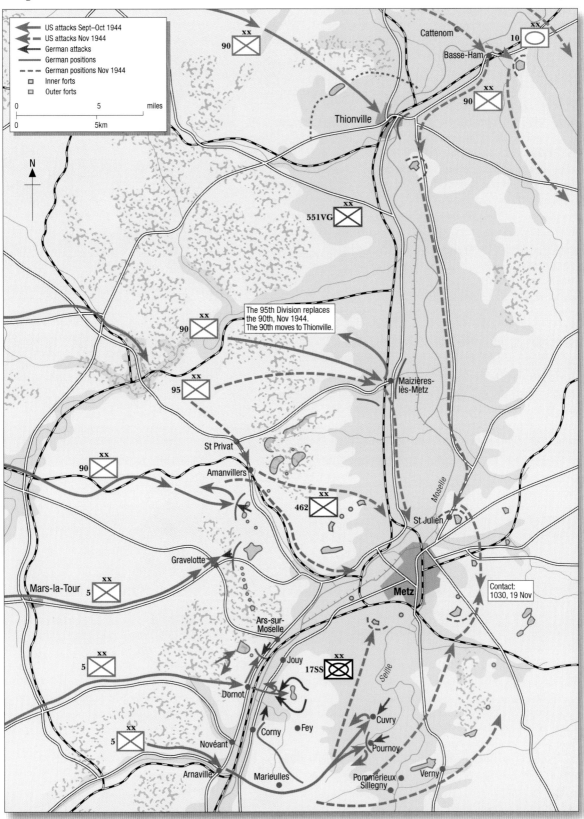

Legend:
- US attacks Sept–Oct 1944
- US attacks Nov 1944
- German attacks
- German positions
- German positions Nov 1944
- Inner forts
- Outer forts

0 — 5 miles
0 — 5km

N

90 xx

10

Cattenom

Basse-Ham

Thionville

90 xx

551VG xx

The 95th Division replaces the 90th, Nov 1944.
The 90th moves to Thionville.

90 xx

95 xx

Maizières-lès-Metz

St Privat

90 xx

Amanvillers

462 xx

St Julien

Moselle

Gravelotte

Mars-la-Tour   5 xx

Metz

Contact:
1030, 19 Nov

Ars-sur-Moselle

5 xx

Jouy

17SS xx

Seille

Dornot

Corny   Fey

Cuvry

Novéant

5 xx

Pournoy

Arnaville

Marieulles

Pommérieux
Sillegny

Verny

significantly delayed Lieutenant-General Patton's advance to the Rhine. Patton hardly gave the forts a second thought and looked upon them as a small bump in the road to Berlin. But in the end their strategic position and the steadfast determination of the German defenders would hold up the American Third Army in front of Metz for two months, and give Patton what is arguably his only defeat of the war.

World War I and the interwar years

The forts of Metz and Thionville saw very little action from 1914 to 1918. They were fully manned at the outbreak of the war and their garrisons reduced over the ensuing months as attrition warfare took its toll. The Germans did not expect a direct attack at Metz but they were fully prepared if one should come.

On 21 August 1914 the two mobile 15cm SLB guns of Feste Wagner fired on Nomeny in support of a German attack to seize the Butte de Xon. Feste Luitpold's guns also supported the attack. Further west the Fifth Army established the St Mihiel Salient and the front stabilized for the next four years. During the war some forts served as shelters for troops on their way to the front. In 1918 the St Mihiel and Argonne offensives by the Americans proved to be the end of the German garrison at Metz and on 11 November 1918 the forts were abandoned to the French. Between the world wars, the forts served as storage depots.

As tension with Hitler increased, the Moselstellung was incorporated into the Maginot Line. In 1939, as war loomed once again in Europe, the Maginot Line fortress artillery unit, the 165e Régiment d'Artillerie de Position, was assigned to defend Metz. The regiment was broken into nine batteries and assigned to the Groupes Fortfiés Yser, Marne, Driant, Verdun, Lorraine, François de Guise and Jeanne d'Arc, and the infantry works of Chesny Sud and Fort Plappeville. They manned most of the turret guns, plus mobile 75mm mortars, 280mm and 370mm pieces, and 75mm anti-aircraft guns.

OPPOSITE
A depiction of XX Corps' offensive to encircle Metz – September–November 1944.

LEFT
US Forces from the 5th Infantry Division and 7th Armored Division crossed the Moselle River at this location on 8 September 1944. The railway bridge in the background leads across the tracks from the village of Dornot. (Author's collection)

Wehrmacht soldiers posing on a 10cm long-barrelled gun at Metz or Thionville. German soldiers took a large number of photographs of their wartime experience. Many photos ended up in personal photo albums where they were sold by descendants many years after the death of the veteran. (Marc Romanych)

The 2e Régiment du Génie refurbished the motors and installed new motors and equipment in some of the forts. The 18e Compagnie of the 68e Régiment du Génie repaired the perimeter defences.

World War II

The German attack on France and the Low Countries began on 10 May 1940. On 13 June, the Metz forts were evacuated (although nearby Maginot Line fortresses remained garrisoned and combat active) and Metz declared an open city. During the war much of the equipment was stripped from the forts by the Germans and used in the defences of the Atlantic Wall and the Ruhr industrial region. The forts served once again as storage depots for war *matériel*, including submarine torpedo warheads. (In 1944 a P-47 pilot returning from a mission noticed a German convoy of trucks on the road leading to the Ouvrage de Mercy at Groupe Fortifié Marne. He dropped his only remaining bomb and it hit one of the trucks, causing an explosive chain reaction that continued to the torpedo stockpile inside the fort. The huge concrete barracks was completely destroyed, leaving a large crater.)

The area was relatively quiet until Patton's Third Army broke out from Normandy in 1944 and raced east towards Germany. By the close of August the Third Army had captured the Champagne region and passed easily by the Argonne Forest without a shot fired. Many of the higher-ranking officers in Third Army had fought in a very different Argonne in 1918, and their memories of that time were fresh. On 31 August, Patton seized Verdun. Third Army's objective was to advance into Germany via Metz–Saarbrucken–Frankfurt and strike at the Ruhr. When fuel supplies began to run out, Third Army was forced to pause on the Meuse. When petrol supplies dwindled Patton was given the option of advancing to the Meuse if 'advisable and feasible'. Patton had enough fuel to allow some armour to cross the Meuse, and XX Corps established a bridgehead beyond the river.

Third Army was comprised of XII Corps under Major-General Manton Eddy, and XX Corps under Major-General Walton Walker. Both were veterans of the battles of Château Thierry, St Mihiel and the Argonne Forest. XX Corps, which would be tasked with the reduction of Metz, included 7th Armored Division (Major-General Silvester), 5th Infantry Division (Major-General Irwin), and 90th Infantry Division (Brigadier-General McLain). Air support would come from XIX Tactical Air Corps, which was still engaged at the time in the destruction of Festung Cherbourg.

After the Allied breakout from Normandy Hitler ordered his forces to hold their ground, even if surrounded. Still, the German Army continued to retreat towards Germany. In early September his retreating armies were ordered to hold in front of the West Wall to allow time for it to be rearmed. Patton encountered elements of General der Panzertruppen Otto von Knobelsdorf's First Army at Metz. It was a shell of a force, consisting of nine infantry battalions, two field gun battalions, three flak battalions, ten 75mm anti-tank guns, the 3. and 15.Panzergrenadier Divisionen and the 17.SS-Panzergrenadier Division. Two battalions of the 17.SS-Panzergrenadier Division were ordered to form an outpost line at Metz. The forces in front of Metz and Thionville were part of

LXXXII Corps of First Army under Generalleutnant der Waffen-SS Herman Priess. (Designation of this unit changed on 7 September to XIII SS Korps.) His forces defended Metz with the 17.SS-Panzergrenadier, 48.Infanterie and the 559.Volksgrenadier divisions, along with Division 462, made up of students from the nearby Fahnenjunkerschule (Officer's Candidate School), and Unterführerschule (NCO School).

In planning for the drive to the Rhine, Metz and Thionville were considered 'intermediate objectives' for the Third Army. They were assigned to the 5th and 90th infantry divisions, while 7th Armored Division was to advance beyond Metz to the Saar. Before fuel supplies arrived, Patton decided to push ahead as far as possible beyond the Meuse bridgehead with his reconnaissance elements. On 1 September, the reserve Combat Command (CCR) of 7th Armored Division seized a large supply of fuel at Étain, along the Metz–Verdun highway. This allowed divisional reconnaissance patrols to move to the Moselle where they reported enemy forces moving into Metz. On 4 September, fuel began arriving and the 3rd Cavalry Reconnaissance Squadron moved east and reached the heights above Thionville to look for a place to cross the Moselle. Patrols reported German defences strengthening and well developed. A cavalry patrol approached Arnaville on the Moselle south of Metz, and moved north along the river. They found a fording site at Ars-sur-Moselle, but were halted by German infantry. Major-General Walker's strategy was to use the 7th Armored Division to spearhead an assault on the river crossing to make a way for the 5th Infantry Division.

XX Corps found the Germans in a very strong defensive system to the west of Metz. The German intention was to make a stand using their fortifications. Third Army knew very little about these defences and they had no detailed relief maps. Most of the forts lacked working guns, munitions and fire control; many had no guns at all. Only Feste Kronprinz (commonly called Fort Driant by the Americans) had its guns functioning on 6 September. Communication between the forts was poor. The cadet school students, considered the elite of the Germany Army, held the line of the western salient. They were chosen for their potential and leadership ability and the morale of the garrison was excellent, due to the physical strength of the forts and the excellent ground they possessed.

The western salient ran from Arnaville to Mondelange on the Orne River, 16km north of Metz. To reach the Moselle, US forces had to negotiate three difficult defiles, the Rupt de Mad, the Gorze and the Mance ravines. The most dangerous passage was the Mance route that passed between the Bois de Vaux Plateau and the Bois des Oignons, both dominated by Fort Driant and its annex, Batterie Moselle. Driant was the key to the southern position. In the centre, Feste Lothringen and the Kellerman works dominated the plateau in front of the village of Amanvillers. The small works in the Canrobert position defended the north flank.

At noon on 6 September, the 5th Infantry Division advanced in three columns, one moving from Conflans north to Verneville opposite Amanvillers and St Privat. There they encountered units of Division 462 entrenched in the German forts. The two other columns advanced from Mars-la-Tour to Gravelotte and Chambley to Gorze, where they encountered elements of 17.SS-Panzergrenadier Division. The area had been the scene of the bloody battle of Gravelotte that took place 74 years before and had forced French forces back into Metz.

On the same day Combat Command B (CCB) of 7th Armored Division and the 23rd Armored Infantry Battalion fought their way down to the river to a

10cm battery

15cm battery

Barracks R

Barracks S

US attacks

German counterattacks

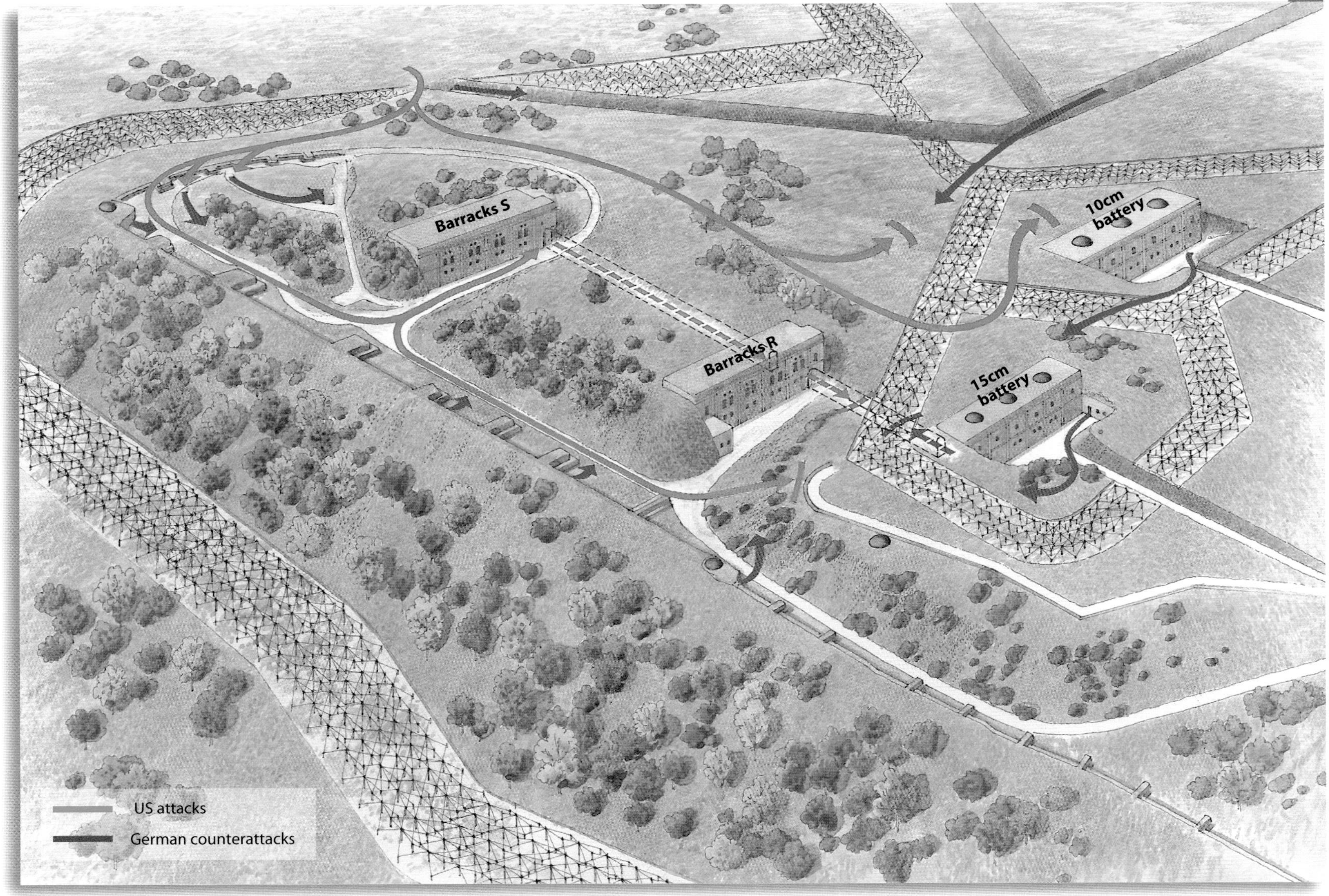

small hamlet called Le Chêne, a few hundred metres north of the village of Dornot. As dawn approached, lead elements came under fire from the guns of Fort Driant and several armoured vehicles were destroyed. The armour pulled back and the next day the 5th Infantry Division was ordered to move through 7th Armored Division and cross at Dornot. On the 8th the crossing was made by assault boat and a small bridgehead was established in the woods on the east bank. A major crossing was made impossible by artillery fire from German 88mm flak guns and Fort Driant's artillery, which kept up a relentless barrage. US 105mm howitzers were moved in to support the bridgehead and in the late afternoon companies F and G of 2nd Battalion, 11th Infantry Regiment, crept towards the Groupe Fortifié Verdun (forts Sommy and St Blaise), known to the Germans as Feste Graf Haeseler. A sniper shot and killed the commander of Company F. They reached the wire of the fort, cut through it, and approached the ditch. Meanwhile, 2.Bataillon of 37.SS-Panzergrenadier Regiment swept in on both flanks and began to filter to the rear of the two companies. With the approach of the 37.SS-Panzergrenadier Regiment, the Americans pulled back towards the river and dug in to a horseshoe-shaped line of foxholes in the woods between the river and the highway that ran parallel to it. German mobile flak guns patrolled the road and strafed the woods, but didn't attempt an assault on the position.

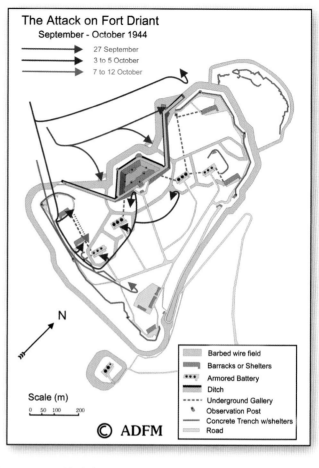

The Attack on Fort Driant
September – October 1944

27 September
3 to 5 October
7 to 12 October

N

Scale (m)
0   50 100   200

© ADFM

Barbed wire field
Barracks or Shelters
Armored Battery
Ditch
Underground Gallery
Observation Post
Concrete Trench w/shelters
Road

This map shows the progression of the battle that took place at Fort Driant in late September to early October 1944. The Americans were able to penetrate into the centre of the fort but could not get into the tunnels below. As a result they were vulnerable no matter how much of the surface they were able to occupy, as the Germans could launch surprise assaults from the numerous exits to the surface from the tunnels below.

Forces in the Dornot bridgehead were withdrawn on 10 September after a new crossing location was found a few kilometres to the south at Arnaville. The 1st and 3rd battalions of the 10th and 11th infantry regiments crossed at Arnaville and headed in the direction of Corny-sur-Meuse. The crossing and advance were under continuous bombardment from Fort Driant and a total of 40 other German artillery pieces around Arnaville. The objective was a ridgeline beginning at Hill 386 between Arry and Corny-sur-Moselle. However, because the US had no maps of the area further to the east, they were unaware the Germans had set up on Hill 396, about a kilometre to the east, which commanded Hill 386. The Americans became pinned down. Bridge building at Arnaville was difficult as artillery shells from Fort Driant continually damaged the bridging equipment. CCA, 7th Armored Division, crossed the river on 16 September and was attacked by the now functional guns of the Verdun group.

E   THE DEFENCES OF FORT DRIANT

The south-east quadrant of Fort Driant where most of the fighting took place. US troops entered between the ditch and wire and proceeded along the top of the fort, only to be counterattacked from within the tunnel system beneath the fort. Engineers were unable to destroy the concrete bunkers and the armoured doors. Troops eventually entered Barracks S and proceed to Barracks R by tunnel. A major battle took place in the tunnel between Barracks R and the 15cm battery.

The 5th Infantry Division was ordered to widen the bridgehead and open up a gap for 7th Armored Division to pass through and link up with the 90th Infantry Division north of Metz. The 5th Infantry Division eventually broke out of the bridgehead despite persistent German counterattacks. They were ordered to head north-east, cross the Seille, then the Nied and approach Metz from the south. In front of them lay the advanced line of hundreds of pillboxes built in 1916 to the south of Metz's main fortress line. Beyond the pillboxes, trenches and wire were Feste Wagner, Feste Luitpold and Feste Von der Goltz, plus the smaller infantry works of Chesny Norden and Süden.

On the 18th, concentrated attacks were launched against the Seille position. A break in the weather allowed US aircraft to drop napalm bombs on Feste Wagner to quieten its guns. Attempts to reach the Seille and the small villages astride it were stopped all along the line, as anti-tank guns and machine guns opened fire from the bunkers. On the 23rd the offensive in the 5th Infantry Division sector was halted.

To the north-west, the 2nd Battalion of 11th Infantry Regiment, 90th Infantry Division, attacked to the east of Gravelotte and came upon German bunkers, the outer works of the heavily defended fortress line of Fort Jeanne d'Arc and the smaller works to the south. On 9 September, Task Force McConnell, made up of elements of the 2nd Infantry Battalion, advanced out of St Privat towards Amanvillers. After a short distance along the Amanvillers road they came under fire from the Kellermann Works. Meanwhile, the 1st Infantry Battalion to the north found itself pinned down by the guns of Feste Lothringen. US artillery replied but had no effect against the armoured turrets. The 3rd Infantry Battalion attacked and was repulsed by bunkers at Moscou Farm, and Feste Leipzig checked the 2nd Infantry Battalion's advance. US losses, killed and wounded, were in the hundreds. The CCR was sent to flank the enemy position but was checked by the Fèves Works. Every US advance was checked by the German counterattacks from their defences in the fortress line. On the 14th the 2nd Infantry Battalion's attack was called off. After further battering, including being held up by a single bunker, the entire offensive was called off on the 17th.

Further north, on 10 September, the 357th and 358th infantry regiments of the 90th Infantry Division pushed towards Thionville, passing through the undefended Maginot Line at Aumetz. On 12 September they reached the heights above Thionville, finding Feste Guentrange abandoned. (Oddly, instead of studying the fort, an act that could have been useful later, they sabotaged the guns and moved on.) Upon seeing the US troops in the hills, the German forces withdrew to the east bank of the Moselle opposite Thionville, blowing up the Moselle River bridges on the way. At this time, even if they succeeded in a breakthrough of the defensive line, the 5th and 90th infantry divisions could not move to encircle Metz since the gap between them was too wide and the continued possession of the forts of the western salient threatened their flanks. By the end of September, Third Army's attack to take Metz had bogged down into a stalemate.

In October the emphasis of the Allied offensive shifted to the north to the 21st Army Group in Belgium and Holland, and Third Army was put on the defensive. Patton decided to continue local attacks with the goal of driving a wedge into the Metz forts by capturing the forts in the west and south-west, Fort Driant being the most important. Major-General Walker was not impressed by the fort and ordered 2nd Battalion, 11th Infantry Regiment, to prepare to attack it on 19 September. Fort Driant was tactically important to the Germans

in that all artillery in the southern sector was directed and controlled from observers on its heights. Furthermore, along with its annex, Battery Moselle, it could sweep the Moselle Valley with artillery fire in both directions. As the Americans assembled in the woods below Driant they could see nothing of its fortified works accept for the gun turrets, the tops of the barracks, and some observation points. Most of the fort was masked below ground level. The size of the garrison was unknown. Just prior to the attack, engraving plates with plans of the forts had been found in Lyons and were rushed to the scene, but provided little additional help.

At 1415hrs on 27 September, 2nd Battalion, 11th Infantry Regiment, jumped off after an initial air and artillery barrage. Fort Driant's guns were silenced only briefly and opened fire as soon as the shelling stopped. E Company moved out from the south under the cover of a smoke screen. G Company and the 818th Tank Destroyer Company followed. The Germans opened up immediately from the sentry posts with small-arms fire, machine guns and mortars. The Americans encountered the wide belt of barbed wire on the perimeter of the fort. They quickly became pinned down by interlocking fields of fire and were unable to move forward. US 155mm howitzers and tank destroyers had no effect against the forward pillbox defences. After the failure of the initial attack, the assault was halted at 1830hrs and the troops withdrew to the start line.

The attack resumed on the 29th. Engineers brought in tank bulldozers to fill the fort's ditch and 'snakes', long lengths of pipe filled with explosives, to blow paths through the wire. However, the snakes bent and broke and the bulldozers encountered mechanical difficulties. Despite the technical difficulties, the infantry attack proceeded against the south-west and north-west points of the fort. Company E, attacking the north position, was hit immediately by

XX Corps' officers planning the attack on Fort Driant. The photo was taken inside one of the small interval shelters built during World War I to the south of the city of Metz. The attack was planned to reduce the power of the fort to control and observe the entire south-west front and crossings of the Moselle south of Metz. (National Archives and Record Administration, 319G)

The US attack on Fort Koenigsmacker, 9 November 1944

artillery fire. They had to dig foxholes for cover and were pinned down for the next four days. Company B attacked in the south, found a way around the southern tip of the ditch and through the wire and was able to gain a foothold in that area.

As evening fell, the Germans counterattacked from the fort's maze of tunnels and trenches. The Americans would clear out a position only to be hit from the rear by Germans appearing from the vast network of tunnels under the fort that connected the works together. Engineers tried to blast their way

The tunnel in which several days of fighting took place between US and German troops in the battle for Fort Driant in October 1944. The tunnel connected Barracks R in the south-east corner of the fort with the 15cm armoured battery. (Author's collection)

F THE US ATTACK ON FORT KOENIGSMACKER, 9 NOVEMBER 1944

Companies A and B, 358th Infantry Regiment, 90th Infantry Division, having crossed the Moselle River, assault a key position in the line of advance of the XX Corps. Rifle squads (A) approach the wire entanglement, while mortar teams (B) provide heavy support to the attack. Squads (C) pass through areas of the wire that have been blown by combat engineers (E) who now set explosive charges on the concrete shelters and barracks (J, K).

Squads approach (D) and occupy the forward trench positions (F), surprising the German defenders from the 19.Volksgrenadier Division who are exiting from their shelters to take up defensive positions (H) and begin to set up mortars to shell the trenches. Meanwhile the four 10cm long-barrelled guns in the armoured gun battery (I) fire at US troops advancing to the north.

into the bunkers, but the explosives had no effect on the concrete surfaces and armoured doors. They were finally able to capture the southernmost barracks (which they called a 'bunker'), identified as S on the maps. They moved on to capture Barracks R and found a tunnel leading from there in the direction of the 15cm howitzer battery. If they could reach this battery through the tunnel they thought they might be able to find their way into the central part of the fort, something they had been unable to do on the surface. Engineers blew open the first armoured door and found the tunnel blocked by debris. (Each time they set charges the carbide gas from the explosives poisoned the air and the men in the barracks, including the wounded, had to be cleared out of the block.) The engineers cleared the debris from the tunnel. They moved further down the tunnel only to encounter a second armoured door. They managed to blow a small hole through the second door and were immediately shot at by German snipers and machine guns set up further down the tunnel. The Americans set up a sandbag berm and the two sides exchanged fire. They were unable to advance any further.

By 9 October, after suffering the loss of 21 officers and 485 men, the US attack was called off. It was determined that the Germans had every position on the fort zeroed in. The Verdun forts provided supporting fire as the guns of Driant couldn't fire on forces attacking it, with the exception of a couple of guns that were lowered to a negative angle to rake the tree line over the US soldiers' heads. A US 8in. howitzer battery firing from nearby on Fort Driant landed eight direct shots on one of the gun turrets. After the howitzer stopped firing, the same turret, undamaged except for a few nicks, opened fire on the US battery. The defeat was very difficult to accept for XX Corps and Third Army, but they learned many lessons about how to assault a fortified position. Third Army, waiting for the results of the campaign in northern Europe, now paused to regroup and to await reinforcements. In November, they would mount what they hoped would be the final assault on Metz.

The plan of attack remained unchanged. 90th Infantry Division was to cross the Moselle north of Metz at Thionville and 5th Infantry Division would cross and encircle Metz from the south to link up with 90th Infantry Division to the east. The difference was the arrival during the pause of the 95th Infantry Division and the 10th Armored Division. The 95th Infantry Division would contain and then drive in the western salient while the 10th Armored Division would swing to the left of the 90th Infantry Division into Germany. Another change would be avoiding direct assaults on the large fortifications. With the exception of a very cautiously planned assault to neutralize Feste Koenigsmaker, the remaining forts would be invested rather than reduced and seized. D-Day was set for 7 November.

The weather throughout most of November was terrible. Seven inches of rain fell, swelling the Moselle River over its banks. However, this didn't stop the 90th Infantry Division from crossing at Cattenom opposite Feste Koenigsmaker on the night of 7 November. It was vital to eliminate the threat the fort posed to US forces moving along the ridges that ran past the fort to the south-east. The 1st Battalion, 358th Infantry Regiment, was tasked with taking the fort. On 9 November artillery fire from Fort Koenigsmaker disrupted the bridging operations that were necessary to bring tanks and heavy equipment across the river. Companies A and B of the 1st Battalion, 358th Infantry Regiment, crossed over on the 9th and approached the fort from below. They cut through the wire and completely surprised the German sentries. The fort was garrisoned by the 74.Volksgrenadier Regiment, 19.Volksgrenadier Division, who, when the alarm was finally raised, rushed out of the tunnels to counterattack with mortars. The mortar and long-range gunfire were directed from the observation post on top of the fort. The heavy guns kept up a continuous barrage against troops moving past the hilltop. A platoon from the 315th Engineer Combat Battalion set about the destruction of the observation posts and the infantry exits. They placed satchel charges against the doors and on the stairs, closing off the exits and preventing the type of sneak attacks that took such a toll at Fort Driant. Ventilation shafts were doused with gasoline and set on fire with thermite grenades or TNT. By nightfall, the US soldiers were well established on the western edge of the fort but they had yet to silence the guns. On 11 November a patrol of 145 Germans sent to reinforce the garrison was ambushed. Feste Koenigsmaker was now completely surrounded. The German occupants attempted to evacuate the fort but were cut off and surrendered. German losses defending the fort were about 300 dead or captured.

On the afternoon of the 11th, with increased freedom of manoeuvre, US forces moved towards Feste Illangen opposite the city of Thionville. As the advance elements approached the fort, a German soldier came out with a white flag to discuss terms for evacuation of the fort. A US officer demanded the fort's immediate surrender but the Germans refused. 155mm and 240mm howitzers kept up a steady bombardment of the fort throughout the night, and an assault force blasted the bunkers with TNT. The fort surrendered the next day at 1045hrs. All of the forts of Thionville were now in US Army hands and the 90th Infantry Division moved south towards Metz.

To the west of Metz the 95th Infantry Division inched its way through the western defences, capturing the road between Fort Jeanne d'Arc and what the Americans called the 'Seven Dwarfs' (the infantry positions from St Hubert to Marival). The guns of forts Driant and Jeanne d'Arc were still operational, German resistance was stiff and there was a dangerous moment when some units were cut off. The 95th Infantry Division eventually overwhelmed the Germans and was able to leave the forts behind and move into Metz. The situation was much the same in the 5th Infantry Division sector, and the stubborn Germans had to be dislodged from the Frescaty airfield near Fort St Privat. The 90th Infantry

US Troops raise the American flag atop Fort St Blaise, December 1944. The battle for the fortress of Metz was a gruelling, three-month campaign. The last fort surrendered in mid-December. (National Archives and Record Administration)

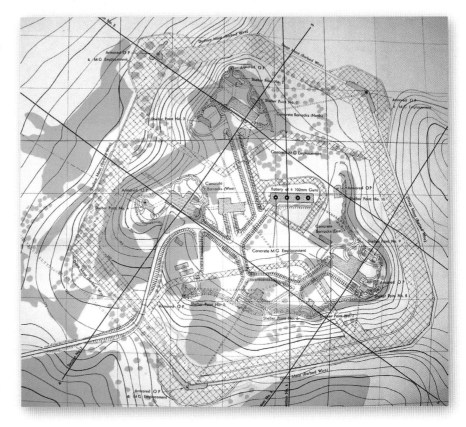

A US Army Corps of Engineers map of Feste Koenigsmaker. After the November battle, the engineers were left to explore and map the German forts, in collaboration with the French. Similar maps showed the location of craters from Allied bombing of the forts. (National Archives and Record Administration, 319G)

OPPOSITE

This photo was taken in November 1944 to study the effects of the bombing of Feste Luitpold (Fort Yser). The Americans did not attack the fort. The Germans evacuated the fort in November. In the centre is the armoured battery that was completely destroyed by US engineers to test the vulnerability of the German concrete. The exact details of this study are unknown. (Marc Romanych)

BELOW

Fort Driant's central barracks in December 1944 after the battle. Compare this caponier with that of Feste Kaiserin on page 58. Note also the concrete reinforcement of the lower half of the façade. (National Archives and Record Administration)

Division met with some resistance from Fort St Julien. However, when they approached the fort and blasted open the iron door guarding the entry postern with a 90mm high-velocity gun mounted on a tank destroyer, German resistance ended quickly.

At 1030hrs on 19 November, the 10th Infantry Regiment linked up with the cavalry squadron of the 90th Infantry Division, and Metz was completely encircled. The city surrendered later that day. One by one, the nearby forts also surrendered: Verdun – 26 November; St Privat – 27 November; St Quentin – 6 December; Plappeville – 7 December; Driant – 8 December (Fort Driant surrendered at 1545hrs to the 5th Infantry Division); finally, Fort Jeanne d'Arc fell on 13 December, two months and 12 days after US reconnaissance patrols first glimpsed the Moselle River.

The final, successful envelopment of the position was attributed to combined ground forces and skilfully planned operations marked by thorough execution. Losses in September and October made the US forces wary of operations that would cause high losses and dramatic failure, such as the defeat at Fort Driant. This prompted a slow, cautious approach using overwhelming superiority in manpower, guns and tanks. The German forts of Metz, even under conditions of decay and lack of

FC – Flanking casemate (counterscarp)

FC

Western armoured Battery

Ditch

FC

observation. cupola

Principal infantry works

Picket shelter

Eastern armoured battery (destroyed)

FC

Wire belt

Infantry works Only

FC

FC

FC

manpower, and stripped of weapons, armour and optical equipment, blocked a powerful army, far superior to the French Army of 1914. The Moselstellung had nearly fulfilled the purpose intended by its designers more than 50 years and one world war before.

AFTERMATH

The victory of the XX Corps at Metz did not end the war. Hard fighting continued for six more bloody months, especially the Battle of the Bulge and a smaller offensive in northern Alsace that pushed the Allies out of their foothold on the Maginot Line near Bitche. In a matter of days, after the conclusion of the battle of Metz, XX Corps found itself facing the West Wall, known by American GIs as the 'Siegfried Line'. Would they find well-armed, impenetrable defences similar to the German forts of Metz, or would they find it to have been nothing more than a propaganda tool? The combat experience at Metz taught the US forces a great deal about the proper way to reduce static German defences and it gave them a taste of what they might expect to find in their drive to the Rhine.

Metz also provided US combat engineers with a testing ground. They knew as little about the West Wall as they did the fortifications of Metz. The West Wall was a system of interlocking pillboxes and obstacles similar to the advance positions built around Metz. What US forces would not find, even though the Germans gave the Allies the impression they existed, were large artillery forts like Driant and Jeanne d'Arc. At the end of 1944 the Third Army were much better educated on the best methods for breaking through the defences. The tank destroyers had successfully silenced the guns of the Hackenberg Works, and two large Maginot forts in Alsace, Simserhof and Schiesseck, had been neutralized with methods learned and perfected at Metz. The engineers had taken over that task from the combat soldier, using shaped charges and dynamite in place of infantry or armoured assault. Evidence indicates their methods were perfected at Metz.

On the slopes below Fort Driant was the small annex to the fort called Batterie Moselle. It consisted of an armoured battery for three 10cm guns surrounded by a wire obstacle. The author made a visit to Batterie Moselle prior to the publication of this book and it has been completely destroyed. The ruins can best be described, as the Germans like to describe the forts of Liège, Belgium, after their destruction, as an alpine landscape of huge chunks of concrete now overgrown with trees. On the eastern bank of the Moselle, the western 10cm battery at Feste Luitpold suffered the same fate, although it's still possible to enter the first few rooms of the battery from the access tunnel. An examination of the eastern 10cm battery at the same location shows evidence of damage caused by a series of shaped ('beehive') charge tests on the top of the turrets. Shaped charges were originally used by the Germans against the armoured cupolas and turrets of Fort Eben Emael in Belgium. They directed an enormous amount of explosive force against a small area of the armour, blowing a small hole through several centimetres of steel. The cause of the extensive damage at Feste Luitpold and Batterie Moselle is not known. It is possible US combat engineers did it in November 1944 to test the strength of the concrete. The purpose of the tests may have been to determine which explosives would have the best effects on the concrete and steel of the West Wall. There is an aerial photo of Feste Luitpold taken by Eighth Air Force on 19 November 1944 that shows the damage described above. It's possible, but not probable, that it was caused by aerial bombing or by the Germans to sabotage the fort. The debris is scattered in all directions and there doesn't appear to be the sort of large crater an aircraft would typically leave. A small number of bombs were dropped at Metz by heavy bombers.

After the war, the province of Lorraine quickly returned to French control, as did the German forts. Metz had always been a strategic location for the French Army, and it still is today. A few Moselstellung forts were occupied and used by the French Army, mostly for equipment storage, but also for use as communications and radar facilities. The large area of ground occupied by the forts was also ideal for unit training and manoeuvres, and the land remained under military control. Very few improvements were made to the batteries or casernes. Most of them were left to decay and many were heavily damaged during combat in autumn 1944 and later from neglect and vandalism. The only forts still occupied by the French military are the Groupes Fortifiés Lorraine and François de Guise.

Beginning in 1953, some forts were used by French, US and Canadian forces belonging to NATO. Canada's overseas Air Division Headquarters moved from Paris to the Château de Mercy at Metz in April 1953. The château is less than a kilometre from Feste Von der Goltz (Groupe Fortifié Marne). A communications site was constructed on the grounds of the abandoned *Feste*. A radar station used by the 61st Aircraft Control & Warning (AC&W) Squadron was installed near the château. The Ouvrage d'Ars became home to their Combat Operations Centre (COC) and other military sections.

The Ouvrage d'Ars as it stands today. The white blocks mark the locations of designated parking areas for Canadian NATO forces that occupied this building from 1953 to 1967. (Author's collection)

The 5.3cm flanking casemate of the Seille Trench, Feste Wagner. This casemate housed four 5.3cm Krupp rapid-fire guns, able to fire 20 rounds per minute. Munitions were stored in the rack on the wall to the right. For further details, see the cutaway on page 18. (Dan McKenzie)

The façade of the central caponier of Caserne 7, Feste Kaiserin. The crest belongs to the Kaiserin Auguste Viktoria, wife of Kaiser Wilhelm II. Compare with the stark version of a similar caponier at Fort Driant on page 54. (Author's collection)

The 601st Telecommunications Squadron established a transmitter site at the Ouvrage de Jury. The interior of both locations was given a facelift with the addition of new wall coverings, ceilings, latrines, lighting and communications equipment. New power generators and transformers were installed. There are remarkable photos of the outside of the Ouvrage d'Ars taken in the 1950s (these and many other photos taken by Canadian forces members at Metz can be found on the Pinetree Line's website, http://www.pinetreeline.org/), showing military personnel going to work inside the building, parking their private vehicles in designated spaces in front of a landscaped building. The comparison with the area today is astounding. Following the disbandment of 61st AC&W Squadron on 31 December 1962, the facilities at the Ouvrage de Jury were closed and moved to the Ouvrage d'Ars.

NATO forces were also looking for an air traffic control facility and selected Fort Jeanne d'Arc. It was designated the Moselle Common Area Control (MCAC) and provided approach control service for four United States air forces in European bases plus a flight plan service for the French and Royal Canadian Air Force (RCAF) base at Grostenquin. Moselle Control was responsible for military air traffic control in north-east France, a portion of Luxembourg and some of the area of West Germany. There were Canadian Air Force (RCAF), French Air Force (FAF) and American Air Force (USAF) controllers stationed there.

The RCAF financed initial renovation of the MCAC site. The French government authorized an expenditure of 73 million French francs for further development. The interiors of casernes 3 and 4 were completely refurbished. The floor was removed in Caserne 4 to make way for a large communications control room and for the addition of new electric motors to power the facility.

On the top were the radar antennas and a dog kennel and run for the guard dogs. There was also a large Quonset hut that housed the kitchen and unit dining room. The radio transmitter antenna towers were on the right side at the lower level of the fort. The outside of the fort was surrounded by concertina wire. The receiver site was 300–400m away.

The baking oven at Groupe Fortifié Guentrange – a work of art. A coal fire underneath a series of water-filled pipes produced the heat. Access was at the rear of the oven. The fort is a museum and is open for guided visits. (Dan McKenzie)

The French Air Force maintained a presence at Fort Jeanne d'Arc after the ejection of NATO forces by President de Gaulle in 1967. Some newer buildings were constructed above the old casernes and are still visible today. The French Air Force abandoned Fort Jeanne d'Arc in the late 1990s.

THE SITES TODAY

For the military historian or fortifications enthusiast, there are few areas in Europe more replete with historically significant sites and a variety of fortifications and monuments dedicated to battles from so many different eras.

Metz was a frontier garrison city for much of its history. The Metz/Thionville region is so rich with different types of fortifications that it serves as a classroom for military engineering through the ages. It is nearly impossible to see all of the fortifications in less than a week, and for the individual studying the history and evolution of military engineering a visit is highly recommended. One can see medieval castles, Renaissance châteaux, fortified farms, Vauban and Cormontaigne bastions, early Séré de Rivières fortresses, remains of citadels, the first concrete and steel forts built by the Germans, large complexes of casernes and depots, and the advance posts, casemates and largest works of the Maginot Line. More firepower ringed Metz and Thionville than anywhere in the world. However, the subject of this book being the German forts built between 1871 and 1916, this narrative will concentrate on their current state and what is left to be seen.

As far as modern fortifications go, the Maginot Line has more museums now open for visit than any other fortification system. Unfortunately there are only two Moselstellung museums – Groupe Fortifié l'Aisne (Feste Wagner), south of Metz, and Groupe Fortifié Guentrange (Feste Oberguentringen) next to Thionville – open for visits on the inside. Groupe Fortifié d'Illange (Feste Illingen), also near Thionville, was recently transformed into an open-air museum.

Feste Koenigsmaker has always been a place of interest for the veterans and their families. Over the years some commemorative ceremonies have been held at the fort. Today, access to the fort is forbidden as the terrain is very dangerous. Organized visits are few and far between because of the dangers involved. A proposal is being examined to transform the area into a memorial park similar to Illange. Modifications would include the addition of a parking area, improvements to a footpath leading to the fort, a place to hold ceremonies, the construction of a path around the fort and buildings and a place to view the Moselle Valley.

Of the Moselstellung fortifications, nothing is visible to the visitor unless you know where to look. Even if you were to drive within a few hundred metres of some of the larger works you still would not see anything except 'Terrain Militaire' signs posted on the trees. All of the fortifications are buried in the woods. Indeed, most of the abandoned works are lost in the vegetation.

Groupe Fortifié l'Aisne is located about one kilometre north/north-west of the village of Verny to the south of Metz. The museum is operated by the Association pour la Découverte de la Fortification Messine (ADFM). A visit to the fort is an excellent experience, lasting about two hours. The fort is typically open on weekends from spring through autumn and at other times on demand. The guides are very knowledgeable and truly passionate about the history of the fort and its preservation.

Barracks 4 of the Feste Kaiserin (Groupe Fortifié Jeanne d'Arc). In the background is the defensive caponier with a modern addition on top. This building was used by NATO forces from the 1950s to the 1960s as an air traffic control facility for north-eastern France. (Author's collection)

Forty-eight kilometres to the north, on a hill overlooking Thionville, is Groupe Fortifié Guentrange. I made my first visit to this fort in 1990 and was completely awed by the immense size of the central barracks, arguably the largest of the Moselstellung. At Guentrange it is possible to visit the central barracks, the north battery and the infantry positions and trenches on the north-western face of the hill. The concrete trenches are the most interesting in the area and are in excellent condition. From atop the observation bunker just south of the north barracks there is an excellent view of the city of Thionville and Groupe Fortifié Illange in the distance. The caserne also has a beautifully restored baking oven. Several rooms in the barracks have a collection of artefacts from the German period as well as equipment and photos of the Maginot Line. The fort is well restored and cared for by the members of its association, Amicale du Fort de Guentrange.

Across the Moselle River is Feste Illangen. All of the buildings have been sealed up with concrete. Paved trails surround the buildings and the perimeter and one can spend hours exploring the surface of the fort, including the barracks, armoured battery, infantry trenches and small shelters. Informative signs are posted along the way explaining the features of the fort. It is an amazing feat considering the terrible condition of the fort in recent years.

Two older forts at Metz are open for visits, forts Gambetta and Queleu. The latter is a large community park and the various features of the fort are barely visible through the woods along the paths. The entry is across a causeway over a dry moat and the bastions are visible on either side. Fort Gambetta is also open and the outside can be visited. Hundreds of small bunkers and shelters dot the countryside around Metz and Thionville. Many of these are on private property but others follow walking trails or are alongside the roads and can be found if you know where to look. In the village of Verny a small casemate is disguised as a fountain. North of Thionville, below Garche, a number of shelters can be seen along the Kieselbach Creek which runs into the Moselle. Some have beautiful carvings on the façade. This is the extent of a visit to the German-built forts of Metz and Thionville.

An *escargot* sentry shelter at Fort Driant as it appears today. This is a concrete version. Many others were constructed of metal and scattered throughout the fort. (Author's collection)

Many of the Maginot Line fortifications can be visited in the area. Forts Fermont and Hackenberg are within an hour's drive from Thionville. In addition, the Cattenom Forest boasts the large Fort Galgenberg, Sonnenberg Casemate, and the shelter and observatory of Cattenom. A number of small shelters and trenches dot the edge of the Cattenom Forest salient to the north. The small infantry works of Sentzich and Bois Karre are open for visits. West of Hettange-Grande are the Zeiterholz Shelter and the small Fort Immerhof. Most websites geared towards visits to Metz or Lorraine list the visiting times and most of the forts have their own websites.

BIBLIOGRAPHY

Artelt, Jork, *Tsingtau – Deutsche Stadt und Festung in China 1897–1914*, Düsseldorf, Droste Verlag, 1985

Cole, Hugh M. (ed.), *The Lorraine Campaign – United States Army in World War II*, Washington, DC, Center of Military History, 1993

Decker, Raymond, Léonard, Pierre, Paulin, Jean Marc, and Rhode, Pierre, *Die Feste Wagner – Le Groupe Fortifié L'Aisne*, Association pour la Découverte de la Fortification Messine, Florange, Presses du Tilleul, 2000

Denis, Général Pierre, *La Garnison de Metz 1870/1919*, Metz, Éditions Serpenoise, 1995

Dropsy, Christian, *Les fortifications de Metz et Thionville*, Bruxelles, Dropsy Christian, 1995

Fontbonne, Rémi, *Les fortifications allemandes de Metz et de Thionville 1871–1918*, Metz, Éditions Serpenoise, 2006

Halsey, Francis, *The Literary Digest History of the World War*, New York and London, Funk & Wagnalls Company, 1919

Johnson, Douglas Wilson, *Topography and Strategy in the War*, New York, Holt and Company, 1917

Kemp, Anthony, *Metz 1944 – One More River to Cross*, Bayeux, Heimdal, 2003

Rocolle, Pierre, *2000 ans de fortification française*, Limoges, Charles
      Lavauzelle, 1973

Rolf, Rudi, *Die Deutsche Panzerfortifikation – Die Panzerfesten von Metz und ihre
      Vorgeschichte*, Osnabrück, Biblio Verlag, 1991

Schumann, Maximilian, *Die Bedeutung drehbarer Geschützpanzer
      "Panzerlaffeten" für eine durchgreifende Reform der permanenten
      Befestigung*, Magdeburg, Buchdruckerei von Walter Ochs & Co., 1884

Schumann, Maximilian, *Les cuirassements rotatifs: "affuts cuirasses" et leur
      importance en vue d'une réforme radicale de la fortification permanente*,
      Potsdam, Walter Ochs & Cie, 1885

Steinbach, Matthias, *Abgrund Metz*, München, R. Oldenbourg Verlag, 2002

Truttmann, Philippe and Michel, *Thionville – Fort de Guentrange*, Thionville,
      Gérard Klopp, 1991

GLOSSARY

Advanced armour (*avant cuirasse*) — An outer ring of armour made of cast iron used to provide additional protection for a gun turret.

Battery — A position for artillery, either in the open air on a rampart or built of concrete.

Caponier — A work built across a ditch, on one or more levels, with embrasures to protect it from an enemy attack.

Casemate — An armoured compartment for artillery or small arms.

Caserne (barracks) — A military barracks containing soldiers' quarters and support facilities.

Cavalier — A raised work where artillery was placed to command the surrounding area.

Counterscarp — The inside facing of the outer wall of a ditch.

Ditch — A long, narrow excavation of varying length, width and depth, built to deter an attack on the central part of a fort or works.

Escarp — The inner wall or slope of a ditch.

Fortified group — *Befestigungsgruppe* (*Feste*) – *Groupe fortifié* – A large group of combat elements, including infantry and artillery positions, batteries and shelters, dispersed and conforming to the nature of the terrain.

Glacis — A gentle slope extending from a fortification.

Gorge — The rear face of a works.

Infantry works — *Infanterie-werk* – *Ouvrage d'infanterie* – One or more positions of a *Feste* or placed in the intervals between *Festen* to defend against enemy infantry attack.

Parapet — An earthen or concrete embankment to protect soldiers from enemy fire.

Turret cap — Steel-plated covering in the shape of a skullcap that protects the gun inside the gun chamber. The rounded shape deflects enemy shells.

INDEX

Figures in bold refer to illustrations.